RICHARD NEUTRA

1892–1970

Survival through Design

Barbara Lamprecht

TASCHEN

©2006 TASCHEN GmbH
Hohenzollernring 53, D–50672 Köln
www.taschen.com

To stay informed about upcoming TASCHEN titles, please request our magazine at www.taschen.com/magazine or write to TASCHEN America, 6671 Sunset Boulevard, Suite 1508, USA–Los Angeles, CA 90028, contact-us@taschen.com, Fax: +1-323-463 4442. We will be happy to send you a free copy of our magazine which is filled with information about all of our books.

Editor ▸ Peter Gössel, Bremen
Project management ▸ Katrin Schumann, Bremen
Design and Layout ▸ Gössel und Partner, Bremen
Coordination ▸ Christine Fellhauer, Cologne

Printed in Germany
ISBN 978–3–8228–2773–4

Illustration page 2 ▸ Portrait of Richard Neutra
Illustration page 4 ▸ Emerson Junior High School, 1937–38, Westwood, California

Contents

Introduction

Opposite page:
Chuey House, 1956, Los Angeles, California

In a <u>November 1934</u> issue of the magazine *Progressive Contractor*, an editor described meeting Richard Neutra, calling him "America's best known architect": "He's called by several as 'screwey' talking about Modernism and the Minoans and the Navajos as refining simplicity. . . . When you talk to him, though, he is so plausible and logical that for the life of you, you can't call him crazy. . . . Outside the U.S.A. the man is a genius. . . . I think he shows the foreign articles and a huge book of clippings to bolster up the ideas he is trying to sell rather than to play up Neutra, for underneath the man is sincere and intense. . . . I don't know, maybe the man is running at cross current with all our traditions and best experience. Probably he is slightly cracked, and most of his ideas will blow up with him."

Then the editorial changes tone: "He lives in an ultra-modern experimental residence overlooking Silverlake in Los Angeles . . . in the midst of features which from the outside seem absolutely incongruous in a home, one finds a quiet air of comfort, utility, and a strange sense of detachment from the usual world . . . maybe he can sell new styles of construction to California and greatly improve our construction methods. I hope he does, I like the guy." The unnamed editor wrote with a carefree impudence rarely applied to Richard Josef Neutra, at least in print, but he got the gist of the man.

Within the pantheon of great Modernists, memorable form-making is a requisite. Neutra certainly reconceived the human within remarkable spaces as well as the technologies used to create those spaces. But what made Neutra unique was not an endless search for form <u>but the endless search for the human being</u>. The wellspring of that search was his belief, quite simply, that good architecture—that which reconciles humanity with nature in an "exultant dance of interconnectedness"—heals and that bad architecture—that which alienates the human from nature and from his or her essential naturalness—harms.

Even though his architecture is often construed as being a "machine in the garden," for Neutra the real "machine" in the garden is the human being, whose daily experience could be calibrated through his or her relationship to the environment. That was the architect's task in any setting. "In a courtroom, justice is conditioned by changes in the air qualities of the room and from soporiferous butynic acid and body odors," he wrote.[1]

Neutra grasped the domestic potential of 19th-century Chicago skyscraper construction, a potential he layered not only with an assured sense of artistic composition but also with no less than an obsession with the apparently mundane. The scientist in Neutra specified a bathroom's air requirements but the artist would explode if "humble" objects such as a chrome toilet paper holder, the light switch and the toothbrush holder didn't create a gestalt that not only showed aesthetic intentionality but had a specific impact on the eye and brain and thus on the beholder's well-being. (Neutra did indeed go into a rage when he saw the newly finished bathroom wall at the Monterey Park House he designed for Maurice and Thelma Huebsch in 1958.)

1 Unpublished paper dated February 14, 1969, "Sozialpsychologie und Architektur," trans. Alphonz Lamprecht, Neutra Archives, California State Polytechnic University, Pomona.

Kaufmann House, 1946–47, Palm Springs, California
Mrs. Kaufmann's silhouette hides the pool light.

2 The St. Louis Post-Dispatch, 2 Nov. 1958. University of California, Los Angeles (UCLA) Library, Department of Special Collections, The Richard Joseph Neutra Papers, 1925–70, Manuscripts Division, Collection 1179, Box 203. In the quote, Neutra refers to the Columbia World's Fair and to 1892, the year of his birth; its title was actually the Columbian Exposition of 1893, a fair devoted to "The World's Science, Art, and Industry" according to the official "Book of the Fair." Neutra either was mistaken in the date or he found that fusing the chronological link between him and Sullivan proved irresistible.

Born in Vienna in 1892, he emigrated to the United States in 1923, made his home in Los Angeles and died in 1970 after one of the century's most productive architectural careers. Neutra was reared in the fin-de-siècle atmosphere of social critique, in which 19th-century traditions in linguistics, art, design, music and politics were chewed up and spat out by figures such as Ludwig Wittgenstein, Gustav Klimt, Karl Kraus and Robert Musil. Agnostic, assimilated Jews, his family's world straddled the arts and sciences. The Freuds and Arnold Schoenberg were family friends.

"At the age of eight," Neutra wrote, "I took my first ride on the newly opened Vienna City Transit Line [designed by Otto Wagner, one of Neutra's mentors]. . . . I got enamored with Wagner, his buildings, his fight. . . . As newly appointed Professor of the Imperial Academy of Arts, he opened his course with a manifesto on modern contemporary architecture. Strangely it was the same year when Louis H. Sullivan in the far distant American Midwest built the Transportation building at the Columbia World's Fair and also the year of my birth!"[2]

Despite his admiration for Wagner, tellingly Neutra entered the Vienna Technical University in 1911 for a better grounding in engineering. (Neutra was not only a consummate draftsman but also an artist whose cursory sketches and exquisitely detailed drawings are unforgettable.) He met Rudolph Schindler, his elder by five years, while examining Schindler's graduating thesis. They shared a love for the unrepentant theorist iconoclast Adolf Loos and an admiration for Frank Lloyd Wright; they also shared a common fate: both emigrated to America for when Schindler set sail for that country in 1914, Neutra went to war. It was not until 1923 that Neutra was to follow suit and in 1925 renewed his friendship with Schindler in Los Angeles, where they became brief partners before professional and personal incompatibilities drove them apart.

While Neutra appears not to have been influenced by Loos's style—an ethics-driven eradication of ornament in favor of stripped-down, space-packed masonry cubes—he did absorb the Loosian ideal of "lastingness," of casting off anything superficial, of the nobility in anonymity and rich but unadorned materials. He was certainly infected by Loos's feverish love for America. The Dutch De Stijl movement was a more formal source of inspiration. Neutra experienced first hand its attention to mass and proportion, to composing in point, line and plane, in 1930, when he slept in Gerrit Rietveld's 1924 Schröder House in Utrecht, Holland. Its controlled asymmetry and flexible layering of functions within the same space resonated with the traditional Japanese architecture he had seen the same year. Neutra marveled at the light, thin, small dwellings with their horizontal transitions between spaces with humble wood and paper *shoji* screens, their shimmering translucency. It was a mystery, he mused later, how the houses "fused with their gardens, gardens so spontaneously free of the shackles of dry geometricity."[3]

Finally, one can discern the impact of Wright's Wasmuth *Folios* in the alternating bands of ribbon windows and stucco in his elevation for Gale House, Oak Park, 1909, or in the interlocking volumes and "free plan" of the Willits Residence, Highland Park, 1901. Neutra also admired Ludwig Mies van der Rohe's far more abstract Project for a Brick Villa, 1923.

Besides these important architectural influences there was a unique voice that grounded Neutra's sense of the world and distinguished him from other Modernists. This voice belonged to Wilhelm Wundt (1832–1920), one of the founders of experimental psychology, whose research laid the groundwork for measuring physical sensation. Neutra read his most widely known work, *Principles of Physiological Psychology*, 1874, while at university. Its introduction is entitled "Bodily Substrate of the Mental Life," which recalls Neutra's own approach, linking body and mind, the physiological and the psychological. He came to believe that the human environment must address the senses, defining his philosophy as "biorealism": "bio" from the Greek word *bios*, meaning life, and "realism" because architecture had to take its cue from how humans really behave and how they evolve.

Neutra accepted the hypothesis that the human genetic code evolved on the savannas of East Africa with its open plains interspersed with groups of trees. That hypothesis had dramatic consequences for his designs. Humans had to be able to orient themselves in their surroundings, for which they needed all their senses. The theory provided a rationale for why people need physical contact with nature, even why they need to see the horizon. Embracing such a hypothesis was also one of the reasons Neutra went not just to America but specifically to warm, freedom-loving southern California.

3 Foreword by Richard Neutra in David H. Engel, *Japanese Gardens for Today*. Charles E. Tuttle, Tokyo and Rutland, VT, 1959, p. xiii.

Case Study House #20, 1946–48, Pacific Palisades, California
Dr. and Mrs. Stuart Bailey House, entrance view

Singleton House, 1959, Los Angeles, California
Southeast corner looking into living room

4 *Nature Near: Late Essays of Richard Neutra*, p.11.

Neutra's definition of nature opposed Frank Lloyd Wright's. For Neutra, nature was not "Other" but us. As he wrote in *Nature Near*, a posthumously published collection of essays, "The universe of which we are a part is a dynamic continuum. It extends from the most distant galactic systems into our atmosphere, biosphere, and terrestrial mantle, wafting even deeper into an energetic array of molecular and subatomic events that configure all matter, motion, and mind. Our skin is a membrane, not a barricade. . . . The most remote contours of the cosmos are not just 'out there somewhere' but causally interlaced with the nearest and deepest folds of our interior landscape."[4]

Architecturally, Neutra's "continuum" prompted four practices. First, if there is a "sacred spot" in a Neutra house, it is not the Wrightian hearth. It is the terrace separated from indoor space by a sliding glass wall, preferably a terrace with radiant heating, so that the relationship between indoors and out is charged with ambiguity. Calculating a building's square footage *should* be hard if boundaries cannot be defined. His attempt to knit the indoors and out initially entailed the use of tall windows with low window sills, providing some semblance of protective enclosure.

Later floor-to-ceiling glass sometimes proved detrimental to "shelter." Caroline (Mrs. Henry) Singleton, co-owner of one of Neutra's most photographed houses, recalled that she felt "too exposed" in the house. Her words echo those of the late Arthur Drexler, the Museum of Modern Art's head of design, who suggested in *The Architecture of Richard Neutra* that "it was possible to sit inside a Neutra living room and still wish that one could get indoors."

There is not one, but many recountings of how Neutra would inspect prospective sites on an owner's behalf, even flying across the country to visit them by moonlight, to advise on the best situation for night as well as day, as he did for Alan and Janet Glen's 1960 wood-and-glass house in Stamford, or for Ann and Donald Brown, with whom he tramped around a wooded glen in Washington, DC, with a flashlight in 1967. The need to connect to the site is seen in reflecting pools, outrigger "spider legs," overhangs, fascias that run beyond the building envelope and silver paint. The paint, used for countless yards of wood trim, was not employed so that wood would look like steel. Rather, Neutra wrote often of its capability of "dematerializing" an object to fool the eye.

Second, since humans (and therefore their buildings and technology) were part of nature, there was no need to sentimentalize and pretend that buildings were "grown": "We know children were not brought by the stork. Buildings stand on waterproofed foundations poured in concrete forms from details dimensioned according to engineering computation and contained in a set of blueprints stamped by the building department. Any pretense that buildings are rooted, or draw nourishing chemicals or moisture from the soil into their circulation of sap . . . is poetic metaphor at best and misleading at worst."[5]

Third, the knowledge of our common ancestry meant that human-built environments can possess similar elements. In his 1930 tour of Japan, Neutra observed that, a house for rich or poor shared similar characteristics. Thus, the theory provided him with a rationale for the "generic" dwelling, optimally with 20th-century technology.

Fourth, the architect was a physician who had to know his patient's history. Thus, deep in almost any client file lies a labor-intensive client autobiography, part of the

5 Richard Neutra, "Architecture and the Landscape." Undated manuscript. Op. cit., UCLA Collection 1179.

Norwalk Service Station, 1947, Bakersfield, California

larger "Client Interrogation." One form the architect often used was divided into two columns, one with the heading "Client Need," the other, "Architectural Response"— on which he noted, remarkably, whether that response was to be rendered in plan, in section or in elevation.

These four aspects of "biorealism" were amplified by a fifth element: Gestalt theories of perception, of dark vs. light, of void vs. solid, of figure vs. ground. These provided Neutra with the tools to effect illusions of spaciousness in small structures, for dappling light against a translucent screen, for the "honeymoon moments in life," as Neutra once put it, and, in a larger sense, also to create a more compact, sustainable urban environment.

After the war, Neutra took on odd drafting jobs before being hired by Eric Mendelsohn in Berlin in 1921. While Neutra admired the Expressionist's business acumen, as with Wright, Neutra knew that he would not be taking his particular architectural path. He was after something other than expression alone, though in some of his own work, such as the exuberant 1947 Norwalk Service Station in Bakersfield, or the sweeping facade of the 1942 Channel Heights market in San Pedro,

Dion Neutra House, 1949–50, remodeled 1966 by Dion Neutra, Silverlake, Los Angeles, California

his ability to "accelerate" a line or plane recalls his work with Mendelsohn on the *Berliner Tageblatt* headquarters. But he did make it his job to track down the important figures of architecture along with their buildings, just as he did with Louis H. Sullivan, finding his impoverished hero ill in his shabby hotel room and, fittingly, meeting Wright at Sullivan's funeral. Neutra worked for Wright for three months. Disappointed by his love of masonry (which Neutra regarded as gratuitously heavy) and his use of ornament, he and Dione left. The Neutras arrived on the doorstep of Schindler's seminal North Kings Road House in Hollywood in February 1925, where they lived for five years, assisting Schindler; the two architects also collaborated on a competition for the League of Nations.[6] Neutra worked on *Wie baut Amerika*, 1927, a book championing not design but construction techniques, especially steel, as well as on projects with Schindler and the independent work of Irving Gill, Neutra himself, Schindler, and Frank Lloyd Wright. (Neutra's fantasies about American freedom, the result of his Old-World way of thinking, soured when he saw revivalist cladding "suffocate" the soaring steel skeleton of the 1923 Palmer House in Chicago, on which Neutra toiled as draftsman #208 for Holabird and Roche, Chicago. The book was his opportunity to denounce such "false" practices.) Two years later, the Lovell Health House was built to critical acclaim. By 1932, Neutra was the only West Coast architect to be invited to participate in the watershed "Modern Architecture" exhibition at the Museum of Modern Art, New York.

Beginning in the early 1930s, Neutra refined his formal idiom in a family of details over decades. Metal casement windows remained a stalwart element of Neutra's kit of parts, used for lavish homes or projects as modest as the haunting redwood-clad "Three Small Houses in an Orchard," Los Altos, 1935–39. For interior finishes Neutra preferred monolithic surfaces and hardware-free cabinetry for maintenance ease and because they read as clean planes. The rubbed, waxed Masonite of the 1930s gave way to birch, mahogany and Japanese ash plywood, painstakingly detailed so that wood grain matched even when planes changed.

In general, earlier houses, such as the 1939 McIntosh House, Los Angeles, were conceived as a series of interlocking, minimal boxes. The roof acts as a lid, which does not engage the sky but confronts it as a crisply closed container. In later work, these boxes dissolved into a series of planes and lines dynamically sliding past each other in three-dimensional collages, as in the 1949–50 Dion Neutra/Reunion House, Los Angeles, elegantly remodeled by Dion Neutra, or the 1956–57 Sorrells House, Shoshone.

With the 1941–42 Nesbitt House, Los Angeles, he reinterpreted traditional materials and methods, such as board-and-batten and brick with slumped mortar. These were more difficult to render as crisp International Style compositions and later designs are marked by slower, stronger tempos of post, beam and larger sheets of glass; casement windows were reserved for private domestic areas. In the last two decades of his life, Neutra executed larger public commissions, mostly in partnership with Robert E. Alexander and, later, with his son Dion. In some cases this architecture, especially the large-scale projects, faltered. It lacked the self-confidence that characterizes so much of his mature work, resulting in tentative buildings with an unresolved quality. But with their clear forms, careful siting and interiors reflecting his obsession with user needs, many smaller projects, such as the Eagle Rock Park Clubhouse, Los Angeles, 1953; the Claremont Methodist Church, Claremont, 1959 (Neutra and

Sorrells House, 1956–57, Shoshone, California

6 Neutra would often go to great lengths to make sure codesigners were credited with drawings and in the books he wrote, but often muddied the waters by listing these people together in the front of a book rather than crediting them for specific contributions. In a similar way, when Neutra collaborated with Rudolph Schindler on an entry to the League of Nations competition for its Geneva headquarters in 1926, Neutra's in-laws, the Niedermanns, handled the entry abroad and despite urgent telegrams from Neutra, omitted Schindler's name in the entry, which toured with an exhibition sponsored by the German Werkbund in 1927. Schindler believed Neutra could have worked harder to ensure he was credited. However, Neutra wrote about Schindler's work extensively in *Wie baut Amerika* and in *Amerika. Die Stilbildung des neuen Bauens in den Vereinigten Staaten*. He also included Schindler's name as coauthor of the competition entry in *Amerika*.

Alexander; Dion Neutra designed a new but similar church following a fire, 1969); and the Mariners Medical Arts Center, Newport Beach, 1963, are outstanding.

Moreover, by the late 1960s, the moralistic and orthodox Modernism Neutra represented had lost favor. Post-Modernism and architects such as Louis Kahn, whose poetical, highly personal geometries resonated with an age less convinced by universal styles and which regarded Modernism as pedantic Puritanism, gained hegemony. Today, Neutra's forms—if not his social concerns which drove the form-making—are again ascendant. Even so, his houses continue to be demolished: Ironically, Neutra's genius for choosing the best lots for homes of modest scale and budget make them perfect targets for an American public seeking grander statements. And yet those who spend time with Neutra often find a nuanced architecture, more poignant than pedantic, more flexible than rigid, than they anticipated. The work echoes the man. As critic Drexler wrote, "Beneath [Neutra's] professional optimism was an intelligence more thoughtful, more private, more hesitant, than the certainties of the twenties allowed."

Neutra Office Building, 1950, Silverlake, Los Angeles, California
Rear facade consists of two apartments, one on each floor.

Right:
Sketch for Case Study House "Omega"

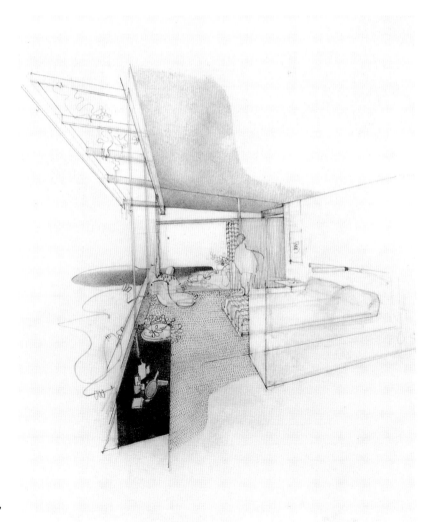

Opposite page:
Miramar Naval Station Chapel, 1957, Miramar, California

14

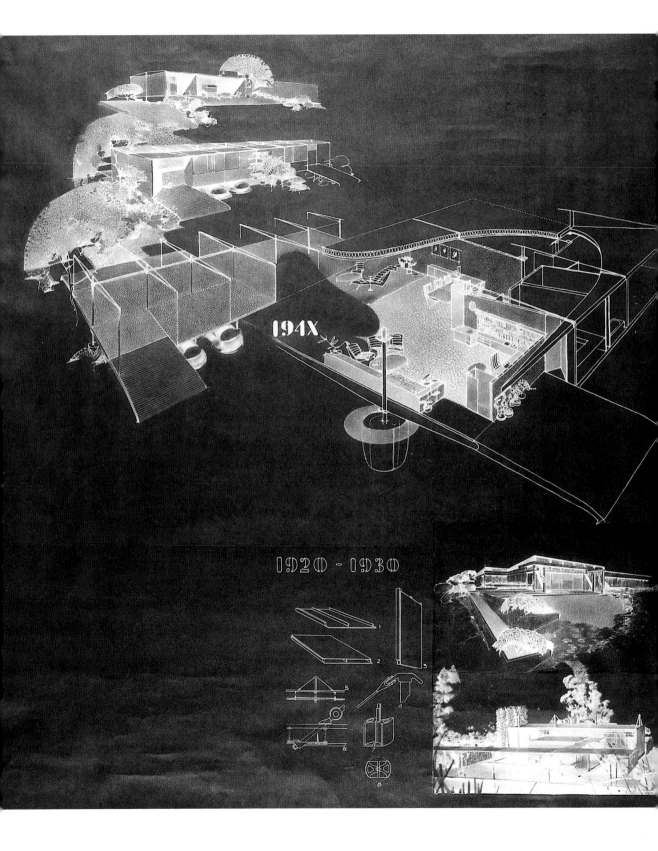

194X

1920 - 1930

1925–1950 · Diatom Series

After World War I ended, Modernists began imagining a heroic future on paper. The images powerfully rendered the shock of the new. Neutra devised his own proposals for hypothetical projects in the 1920s and 1930s to generate ideas on urban design and building technology. These proposals had a direct impact on his work, from unbuilt worker housing to high-end private homes. Rush City Reformed served as his theoretical metropolis. The Diatom Series served housing, exploring not only materials and building systems, but also the modern tract house and the implications of the car. ("Diatom" refers to crushed algae seashells. Even through the 1950s, Neutra held to his conviction that "diatomaceous earth" was the key to creating "steam-hardened earth" akin to lightweight concrete, which could be made into insulated panels called Diatalum for walls and floors. He even attempted to establish a for-profit corporation. The additive eventually proved to be too soft and crumbly, but has many uses today.)

One Diatom design was inspired by the one building representing the promise of American technology: the circus tent. In his 1930 book *Amerika. Die Stilbildung des neuen Bauens in den Vereinigten Staaten* (America: New Buildings of the World) Neutra wrote that that membrane structure with its central post fulfilled all his requirements for "lightness in construction": ". . . in North America, one can view the gigantic tent of the multiple ring circus of Barnum and Ringling Brothers around the middle of the 19th century as the most characteristic architectural production. Developed for erection, dismantling and rail transport almost in the span of hours, in whose framework are arranged stairs, folding seats for many thousand spectators as well as electric and water installations . . . [the way that] the constructive members, such as covers and ropes, function only as mere tensile stresses, and therefore are of minimal dimensions, imparts to the tent also in other ways prototypes for our era which views lightness of construction as an architectural duty and dear to its heart . . ."[1]

Whether he was inspired by the mobile tent or by Buckminster Fuller's 1927 Dymaxion House with its central mast, which he also admired, Neutra used this strategy only once. This was Diatom I, "One-Two," a house typically no more than 1,000 sq. ft. One central unit (three ganged bays 17' 8" x 22' deep with 3'6" overhangs) could be flanked first by one and then another unit. (Reminiscent of Le Corbusier, not only does the sublimely rendered design include a roof garden, but in a 1930s cartoon-like manner, Neutra also depicted gently smudged, rounded ends of autos, peeking out from below the pilotis of the house.) The short walls of the central unit are solid while the long walls are primarily glass from end to end, so the spaces feel bright, open and loft-like, enhanced by a 4' overhang on both sides. Floors, roofs and walls all consist of Diatom panels. A prefabricated kitchen and bathroom made up the mechanical core.

The roof is suspended with tension cables from a series of masts whose central steel columns are set in contrived steel footings anchored in the ground, thus eliminating "over-dimensioned" concrete footings. They were to be adjustable and portable, perfect for instant housing. While these look more like exquisitely fussy watch gears than footings, for Neutra they were quite viable. Though never manufactured, he

1 Richard Neutra: *Amerika. Die Stilbildung des neuen Bauens in den Vereinigten Staaten*, p. 76.

Opposite page:
Diatom I and IV
The center cutaway, Diatom I, shows relationship of structural system of post, tension cables and diatomaceous earth panels to living and parking areas. Note the range of pencil rendering techniques, from disciplined pointillist dots to a smudged style reminiscent of 1930s cartoons, seen on the ends of the cars peeking out from the carports. Diatom IV, anticipating the Tremaine House, bottom right.

Diatom I model and rendering

Opposite page:
Drawings
showing additive and flexible ability of design to
accommodate changing user needs and family
sizes (I, main house; II, a 324-sq.-ft., three-bedroom addition; III, two-car garage).

2 Typed text for unidentified trade journal, June
1950. Along the same lines, in an advertisement
for steel buildings in *L'Ossature Metallique*,
July 1951, he wrote, "Over 30 years I have given
thought to largely or wholly prefabricated
structures, assembled in the field, first by bolting,
then by welding. . . . This handling of steel has
taught me many aesthetic principles. It sharpens
the aesthetic judgment of the architect and
certainly gives him a grand opportunity to him
who wishes to open the interiors of his buildings
to the charms of a well-gardened area and the
beauty of a broad landscape surrounding his
architectural composition."

was granted patents for some of them in the late 1940s. He also designed plants for
manufacturing diatomaceous earth panels, which were published in trade and
architectural journals. He designated production schedules, conveyors, loading . . .
Neutra even worried about union affiliations. "What would traditional carpenters'
unions say?" he asked.

Another, larger Diatom house, Diatom IV, posed an opposite hypothesis. It was far
heavier, built of concrete and wood. At one end, concrete piers acting as spider legs
extended from the ends of the main volume to create a heavily articulated, formal
terrace. Diatom IV's design echoed the elongated volumes of Frank Lloyd Wright's
1910 Robie House in Chicago. With its ventilated openings above lowered spandrel
beams, it was Neutra's reference point for his Puerto Rico classrooms, which in turn
led to his thesis for the Tremaine House.

Neutra never ceased in preaching the gospel of prefabricated houses. He did not
blame the consumer for their love of "tradition, because we don't have a tradition!" he
scorned, referring to the changing parade of house styles. What was needed, he wrote,
is first an understanding of the "intimate relationships in modes of living. . . . What if
we were to build a car the way we build a house? Chaos! The 'rugged individualist' in
each prospective home buyer is flattered into 'expressing himself' instead of squarely
facing the technical and economic facts of life. . . . In spite of ingrained associations of
'my home, my castle,' a minimum dwelling is not and cannot be independent and self-
sufficient. Isolated by itself, it must remain unconvincing as a message for progress
when submerged in an amorphous city stretching on endlessly . . ." His Diatom
models were included in his architecture proposals on paper for "194X," *Architectural
Forum*'s famous postwar housing program in which the "X" represented a future up for
the taking.[2]

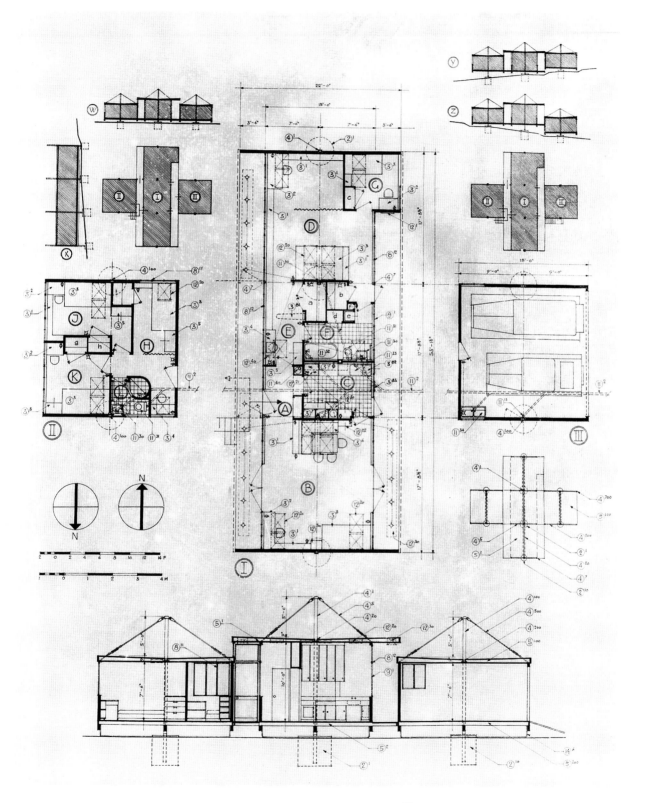

SECTION C-C LOOKING EAST

WEST ELEVATION FROM FIELD

SECTION 5-5 LOOKING NORTH

NORTH ELEVATION

RUSH CITY AIR TRN

LOBBY ELEVATION

LOBBY SECTION

CONCOURSE
PERSPECTIVE SECTION

HANGARS
MODIFIED DYCKERHOFF & WIDMAN CONSTRUCTION

ARRIVING VIEW

RUSH CITY EAST

DEPARTING VIEW

LEHIGH AIRPORTS COMPETITION

1925–1930 ▸ Rush City Reformed
(. . . or, ameliorate, not agitate)

Rush City Air Transfer, 1927

1 The original labels to Rush City Reformed drawings read: "Richard J. Neutra, Architect, collaborating with Gregory Ain, Donald Giffen, Harwell H. Harris, and Ragnhilde Liljedahl" (see *Architectural Record*, August 1930, pp. 99–104). Students at the Academy of Modern Art in Los Angeles where Neutra taught in 1928/29 also helped with the drawings.

2 University of California, Los Angeles (UCLA) Library, Department of Special Collections, The Richard Josef Neutra Papers, 1925–70, Manuscripts Division, Collection 1179, Box 204.

3 Undated private memo titled "1923/1933 Rush City Reformed," Neutra Archives, California State Polytechnic University, Pomona.

4 *Architectural Record*, August 1930, p. 99.

Opposite page:
Lehigh Airports Competition, 1931
In this project the hypothetical work of Neutra and his apprentices is implemented. Except for a little-documented factory in Kuala Lumpur, Malaysia, throughout his career Neutra continued primarily hypothetical but well-considered work on large-scale industrial concerns.

Rush City Reformed was Neutra's contribution to the design of utopian cities. Drawn in the late 1920s by Neutra and his apprentice/protégés, the city they presented showed ideas ranging from tenderness toward the city's alienated at the micro level to the ruthlessness of a totalitarian state at the macro level. Whatever the level, mobility was emphasized: while his city might not have been "rushed," it was definitely equipped for speed. Crisply shaded and shadowed streets, buildings, train stations and airports were all rendered delicately with his fat Siberian soft charcoal pencil.[1]

Besides the house type, Neutra's life-long passion was urban planning. In the fall of 1959, he gave a lecture titled "Human Cities: Is Art Practical?" In it he summed up exactly how he disagreed with Louis H. Sullivan's famous dictum "form follows function." Neutra said, "As a whole our cities are not a success . . . form and pattern are biological necessities. Chaos is the enemy of *Kosmos*, the Greek word for shapefulness. . . . The design of our man-made settings cannot and shall not be reduced to a simple utilitarian formula like 'form follows function' as if form or shape were something static, a rigid cart behind a dynamically functioning horse. Physiologically speaking, the separation of mankind into the tasteful and the purposeful has little meaning. The nature in us is whole and not split . . . it would be hard to say where a tree stops being utilitarian and functional and where it begins to be beautiful. Any such dualism brings us to a blind alley." Neutra observed that as cities have sprawled, traffic problems have only worsened, leading to "irrational commuting," wasting resources and destroying community.[2]

Neutra, of course, was not alone in creating utopias. Ville Radieuse by Le Corbusier and Broadacre City by Frank Lloyd Wright are obvious other examples. But Neutra argued that his solution was based on real conditions, "not an abstract and theoretically rigid scheme."[3] The result was mixed: his prisons are humanized with glass ceilings, skylights, swimming pools and recreation areas, whereas his apartment high rises are chilling in their relentless orthogonality, with one rectangular block after another, mile after mile.

Appearance aside, a closer reading of the larger project shows its appeal as a prototype. Neutra analyzed how to allocate the changing needs and spatial requirements of old and young, families and groups, sometimes in high rises but more often in low-rise houses, using labels such as "Night-Spending Persons" (those working the night-shift) or "Space-Taking Groups" (presumably families). While these labels are amusingly eccentric, they were also effective because they show how his questions affected form as well as language. For example, he rejected "terminal" as a label for his air and train stations, arguing that in a modern world people are much more likely to transfer to a different kind of transportation than to "terminate" a journey. Hence: Rush City *Transfer*.[4]

1927–1929 ▸ Health House

Philip and Lea Lovell House

▸ 4616 Dundee Lane, Los Angeles, California

Opposite page:
The famous double-height glassed staircase with the embedded Ford automobile headlight leads from the street/private level down (instead of the conventional up) to the piano nobile.

Looking west from Dundee Drive across the bridge to the hills beyond. The staircase is to the right in the image.

The Lovell Health House is recognized as one of the most important houses of the 20th century. It is the first American residence in steel and is based on the skyscraper technology Neutra devoured as a draftsman and observer in New York and Chicago. Here Neutra broke with the Wrightian box horizontally and vertically. And while the *pilotis* of Le Corbusier's Villa Savoye lift the villa into the air, they do so in using trabeated construction not dissimilar to that of the Parthenon. Neutra's site is so audacious that he needed to conceive the process to construct it. Like an ocean liner at berth, it hovers, tethered over a steep ravine in Los Angeles.

A concrete "gangplank" bridges street and entry. Here one steps into a low-ceilinged, dark wood-paneled space, and then plunges down a large, glass-enclosed staircase into light and modern living, a metaphor taken up on the stair with the embedded Ford headlight, beacon of American capitalism.

The voyage ends on the lowest level with the concrete swimming pool—perhaps the real "living" room, one end anchored in the very womb of the house, the other jutting out over the valley, so that a swimmer moves back and forth between the bright air and the bowels of the building in a dialectic of liberation and protection. In a sense, Neutra has simply upended Le Corbusier's rooftop terrace, now under the house.

The design is further tied to the hill by the pergola and garage, which extend south and hug the slope, but, by placing the house perpendicular to the hill, Neutra ensured views in every direction. However, by locating the master suite at the southwest corner, with the best view but with no western overhangs, Neutra's move incurred the clients'

View from the southwest

1 1977 recorded interview with Gregory Ain by Kathryn Smith, assistant to historian Esther McCoy, Esther McCoy Papers, Archives of American Art, Smithsonian Institution, Washington, DC. Ain went on to be a highly respected architect who advocated low-cost architecture of social concern. It may be important to note that although he disliked Neutra as an employer Ain acknowledged that he learned much from him.

loathing, who said they "roasted . . . it was like an oven," according to Gregory Ain, who worked for Neutra in 1929 and again from 1932 to 1935.[1]

The Lovells were a flamboyant, progressive couple with strong convictions about physical health. Philip wrote a column, "Care of the Body," for the *Los Angeles Times*. Friends of the Schindlers, they commissioned Rudolph to design the seminal 1922–26 Lovell Beach House in Newport Beach. Rumors still circulate as to why Lovell hired Neutra to design first his downtown office for "Physical Culture" and then his city house; Schindler was even a guest contributor on architecture and health to Lovell's column. It may have been Neutra's less earthy approach to quantifying "health" in buildings as well as his more organized building practices that tipped the scale. In any case, by hiring both men Lovell assured his place in history as a significant patron of Modernist architecture. He also realized his own private sanitarium with outdoor exercise areas, and screened porches for sleeping and eating (the latter now enclosed) as well as an 8'-tall revolving cooler to house goods for the vegetarian family. A 52'-long aluminum light trough in the living room and library washes the ceiling and walls with light; in his later works Neutra employed soffits to accomplish the task. At street level the private rooms disintegrate into a warren of awkwardly connected spaces, some with no access to exterior walls. Lacking Neutra's later typical "spines" of rooms, this move, too, bothered Lovell, who complained to Ain, who apparently remodeled some

Second version, circa 1927

In the final, scaled-back scheme, Neutra focused on the house. He pulled the pool out dramatically, strengthened the composition's asymmetry and eliminated the parking area and staircase, bottom right.

of the interior, that "every time I sit down at my desk, someone backs into me [while coming] through the door."

But Neutra was justifiably proud; thousands came to tour and gape after it was completed. The house assured Neutra an international name. Acting as contractor and overseeing 70 laborers, he rose daily before dawn to check the thousands of bolt holes, he wrote. Gangs of three steel casement windows attached to thin vertical metal stays were placed amidst bigger steel members welded to open web steel trusses supporting corrugated metal floor decks. Balconies were in part structurally suspended by the decks. Neutra eliminated hand-mixing concrete in wheelbarrows by designing a 200' wooden shoot for the foundation concrete and lighter Gunite for the stucco, sprayed onto expanded metal mesh with long hoses (which he may have learned from Schindler, who used this technique in his 1924 Packard House). Framing was finished in 40 work hours. The foundation also supported the pool in a steel and concrete cradle that reduced the number of labor-intensive footings needed.

Formally, the white Gunite bands seem arbitrarily to interrupt the framing grid, sliding against each other, sometimes acting as walls, other times as balcony enclosures. Neutra terminated some of these planes with upended parapets; like the ends of Chinese roofs pointing to the sky, they enhance the structure's alert stance and hide the sloped roof.

West end, living room

It involved much custom work. In 1930, Neutra calculated the total bill for the Lovell Health House at $58,672.32; his fee was $5,863. Ain also reported that "as Neutra became more and more famous, Dr. Lovell became more and more conciliatory about the house." Indeed, by 1968, the Lovells were calling Neutra a "genius" and the house a "masterpiece."

Below left:
Upper floor plan

Below right:
Lower floor plan

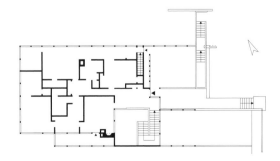

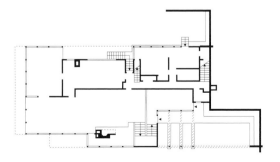

1932 · Van der Leeuw Research House

2300 E. Silverlake Boulevard, Los Angeles, California

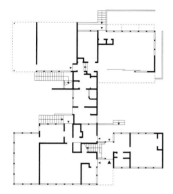

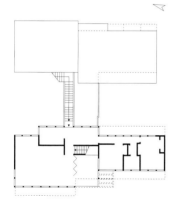

Top:
VDL I lower floor plan

Above:
VDL I upper floor plan

Opposite page:
View north from rooftop penthouse, VDL II

While the Neutra homes VDL Research Houses I and II succeed in their self-appointed task of solving generic problems, they are also intimate family portraits. The houses explore a range of issues. How does an architect communicate his ethics aesthetically? Neutra's response shows how to increase urban density in a city; how to accommodate and layer potentially conflicting uses in a house/office; and how to enhance human vitality through an intimate bond with nature.

With its bands of steel-ribbon windows and white stucco, the new 2,100-sq.-ft. environment (the convention of the word house need not apply) must have stood out boldly in its aesthetic allegiance to European Modernism. Neutra chose a site strikingly similar to that of his patron, the Dutch industrialist Cornelius van der Leeuw, whose house overlooks the Kralingse Plas in suburban Rotterdam. The Neutra design occupies a 60 x 70' plot of land a few hundred feet from Silverlake, both a reservoir and a hilly residential neighborhood not far from downtown Los Angeles. The laboratory for spatial and material research burned down three decades later. A reconfigured VDL II was erected using the existing footprint in 1966.

The name VDL honors the original's benefactor. On Neutra's world tour in 1930, he met van der Leeuw, whose new daylight-infused factories bristled with Modernism. Expecting Neutra to live in an avant-garde house of his own, he was dismayed to see Neutra's modest bungalow quarters in Echo Park while on a surprise visit to Los Angeles. He loaned Neutra $3,000 to build his own house and Neutra raised the rest. The VDL cost less than $8,000, about $105,000 today, or $50/sq. ft.—a meager budget. (Neutra repaid him, with interest, in the late 1940s.) To recall Neutra's words, the brief envisaged a "minimum family dwelling with kitchenette and studio in the rear; a bachelor's dwelling; living quarters with dining room, kitchen, lake porch and separate bedroom wing . . . a workroom basement . . . children's playground, two roof terraces, two garden courts."

To demonstrate density, Neutra shrewdly interpreted newly established building codes, and pushed the two-story structure out to the street line in front and to its full width of 60'. Somewhat echoing Roman atria or Spanish dwellings, an inner courtyard separated the main house and the 677-sq.-ft., $4,300 guesthouse, completed by Christmas 1939. (Here, again, Neutra disingenuously slid past zoning codes, referring to it as a "garage" in order to exploit land typically assigned to setbacks.) Two large glass-and-steel sliding doors open almost the entire west end of the guesthouse living room to the garden. A 200-sq.-ft. ground floor "bridge" of little service and bedrooms for the Neutra boys link the two larger buildings, thus making the overall complex H-shaped.

In both VDL I and II, a short bridge buffers the transition from public street to private life. Just beyond stand two doors. The first, transparent, faces east, providing instant visual access to the landscaped courtyard beyond. The other, to the office, looks north. The adjacent pair highlights the importance Neutra placed on flexible circulation, and, by implication, the freedom afforded users forging their own paths. The ground floor with its neon sign housed the office, secretaries and draftsmen,

Living room

including Gregory Ain, H. H. Harris and Raphael Soriano. These last three well-known architects were all apprenticed to Neutra here, working on Rush City Reformed. The upper floor was devoted to the Neutra family.

Since Neutra could not afford to build in steel but wanted the effect of uninterrupted ribbon windows he altered conventional 2 x 4 wood construction by using larger 4 x 4 wood posts, balloon-framed and milled to receive pairs of steel casement windows. The pairs dictate a crisp module of 3' 3 1/2", a dimensional rhythm that became a standard Neutra feature; on the upper floor he used larger, fixed-glass panes in the same module. Prefabricated concrete joists and suspended slabs provided a fire-resistant floor, an unexpected blessing when archives in the basement survived the 1962 blaze. In good case study house fashion, Neutra persuaded manufacturers to donate materials, such as the aluminum foil insulating three types of wall section varying up to one inch in width, using combinations of rockwool, rigid insulation and lightweight Pozzolan cement. Industrial steel-and-glass folding doors led to the outdoor sleeping porch.

With its low-slung datum lines, aligning the window sills with the low black leather settees lining the outdoor porch, the silvery, dark-toned VDL shimmered with

Street facade

moments of sensuality: the "honeymoon moments in life," Neutra noted, were equally vital "functions." The texture of the leather was offset by the adjacent wainscoting of easily cleaned midnight blue enameled steel panels. Other, more conventionally functional details abounded. Most furniture was built in for maintenance ease. (In VDL II, the high captain's beds can be rolled away from the wall so beds could be made easily. In both renditions bedrooms are small, as compact as ship cabins.) The small, bright kitchen included metal-lined drawers that could be pulled from either dining area or kitchen for discreet food delivery. Overhangs protect the living room from the late afternoon sun. During the day, an aluminum-faced awning at the edge of the 5' overhang shaded the west-facing glass.

Increasingly aware of both physiological comfort and how spatial illusions changed psychological perceptions, he "stretched" space wherever possible. The upper stucco band, for example, flies off the living room volume to frame the entryway below, appearing to elongate the line. Employing one of his favorite Gestalt tools, dark colors were used to make planes recede, light tones to make them come to the fore. A large mirror visually doubled the cramped entry space. He also introduced a trademark, which performed only at night: exterior lights above translucent glazed soffit strips at the edge of the overhang. The light extended living space at night; it also reflected off the glass, providing a "curtain" effect of privacy. The copious glass provided light and views in every direction. The wooden rooftop solarium, a lighthearted volume whose framing ran south to form an elongated pergola, was added to the evolving complex in 1951. Reached by a ship's ladder mounted to the wall of the sleeping porch below, the solarium provided an opportunity to be private but abundantly outdoors.

1933 ⋅ Mosk House

2742 Hollyridge Drive, Hollywood, California

Street facade

1 Neutra's mentor Adolf Loos often spoke about his admiration for the American "humble man in overalls"; in his 1910 essay "Architektur" (in *Trotzdem. Essays 1900–1930*. Innsbruck, 1931, reprinted Vienna, 1982) Loos wrote that "only a small part of architecture belongs to art: the tomb and the monument. Everything else that fulfils a function is to be excluded from the domain of art." Both the Mosk tomb, with its sensitivity toward grief, and the house with its successful features and imperfections, exemplifies Loos's dictum.

Ernest and Bertha Mosk were so dear to Neutra that he designed his only known tombstone for them. Like his houses, the gray granite marker's two interlocking rectangular volumes, one larger than the other, stand apart from noisy neighbors in quiet humility.[1]

At the family's request Neutra spoke at Ernest Mosk's funeral. "I had at last found a client for my prototype for the smallish American home which was so close to my heart. . . . He was the first small man to trust me with all his earthly goods and fate," he wrote in *Life and Shape*. Yet, it was Lona Mosk who had coaxed her adoring father into visiting the Bauhaus while abroad. Her parents hired its local practitioner.

The once gorgeous, now sad, Mosk House is indeed a seminal work of architecture. First, Neutra still employed the horizontal banding rhythms of the International Style, but instead of white stucco, he now spoke with an American accent: shiplap siding, seen again in the far grander 1938 John Nicholas Brown House. Second, Neutra intended the Mosk House to be the first unit of a hillside community that anticipated his built Silverlake Colony two decades later as well as the 1962 Stone-Fisher Platform Houses, which Neutra titled "Steep Hillside Habitations." All demonstrated his three-part requisite of common vocabulary, individual character, and unique site response, in the free-standing American house. (Only the Mosk House was completed, and Neutra named the house not after its owner, as publication convention dictates, but as a prototype, "A Study for Steep Hillside Development," romantically recalling Tibetan monasteries and Thuringian castles.) Third, instead of steel as at the Health House, he used the cheaper VDL strategy that transformed American wood framing know-how. Here a prefabricated concrete joist foundation supports wood posts with diagonally braced wood trusses above and below the window bands. Neutra's "normalised wood chassis," includes 4 x 4 posts whose locations were based on the two-leaf commercial steel casement windows, whose hinges "precisely fit into the rebates of the posts, windows thus forming an integral part of the skeleton." The lower wood skeleton was clad in "waterproofed insulating slabs of 'Puzzolan'," steam-pressed slabs of wood shavings and Portland cement, while interior walls were clad with Masonite or Celotex. Floors and built-in furniture tops were covered with darkish red battleship linoleum.

The house glimmered with two silvers, with aluminum paint for the shiplap and a darker tone below the windows that anchored the exuberant design to the earth. The two-story living/dining volume breaks the one-story envelope on both the west street side and sharp drop-off on the east; in early sketches Neutra planned a rooftop garden. Today not only the shiplap but the silvered fascia flying off the house as a continuous plane in space is gone, amputating the energetic composition that once sailed over land that the Mosks did not own and that later became a city street. Like many 1930s houses, the "public" ceiling was tall, measuring 9', and casements were placed above fixed glass for cross ventilation. However, it shared an unfortunate early feature with its more glamorous siblings, the Lovell and Brown houses: a southwest glass bedroom wing unencumbered by overhangs. One of the sharpest childhood memories recalled by a grandson of the Mosks, James Packer, is that of his Crayola crayons melting into a pool on the floor of the hot, narrow bedroom hall.

Left:
View from the living room, looking to the southeast

Below:
Plan upper floor

Bottom:
Plan lower floor

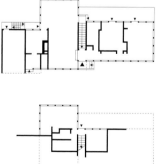

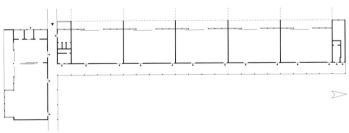

1935 · Corona School
3835 Bell Avenue, Bell, California

"The school is where we hear of facts new to us, where we recreate ourselves, shape our mentalities, our outlooks and social attitudes. . . .We can either enjoy friendly openings into green outdoors or suffer uncontrolled uncanny corners behind cramped furniture . . . and a thousand other psychologically tinged ingredients. No empirically based estimate has yet been made of the magnitude and precise qualities of this major set of environmental influence, but sometimes in our dreams we are pursued, pleased or tortured by recurrent infantile impressions created by them long ago in early terrors or early enjoyments."[1]

"This bolshevik of building has actually converted the School Board of Los Angeles to his idea!"[2]

Between August 7 and August 29, 1934, Neutra drafted seven proposals in ink on vellum for alternative construction systems for an addition to the Corona School in Bell. However technologically experimental the proposals were, it was the innovative spaces he advocated that suddenly made him as famous for his schools as for his houses. The labor-intensive drawings for the five-classroom and two-kindergarten school included "hollow" concrete, a timber frame system and five different steel systems, including the Palmer system used in the Beard House, then under construction. But the final construction method selected was "none of the above." The school with large, sunny, 38 x 24' classrooms was built of conventional stick framing, earning it the nickname "test tube school." It would be the first of many schools he would design or codesign, including the elegant 1938 Emerson Junior High School in Westwood. More typical examples, however, were built in the late 1950s and 1960s with Robert E. Alexander and his son Dion.

Neutra believed in unorthodox educational methods that are standard practice today. Conventional classrooms in a multistory building, he believed, were hazardous to health and to learning with their "well-known sour smell and stale exhalation." A school must prove "a scale of the whole and of all of its parts that is not cruel and foreign to the requirements of childhood," he wrote. Based on intuition (later research confirmed his views), he argued that children in the back of a class needed to see and hear as well as those in the front or they would suffer vision and dental problems, e.g., grinding teeth in frustration. Poor ventilation, he wrote, "produced hot air cushioning around children." Calculated breezes kept students and teachers alert with "less pollutions." He called for research into surfaces for reflectivity and "smell absorption quotient." Our East African ancestors, he stressed, learned best by moving around and by drawing on the ground in groups, not only by sitting in fixed places staring at vertical planes. Nature was necessary, rain or shine.

Architecturally that translated into single-story buildings one classroom wide with operable clerestories on one side and overhangs and one glass-and-steel wall with a 14' 3" sliding door opening on to individual garden patios on the other. His favorite photos and drawings invariably showed movable furniture—with tilting tops and adjustable heights—and children in a semicircle straddling indoors and out.

Though extensively remodeled, his classrooms are still popular with Corona teachers because they are taller and bigger in plan than conventional classrooms.
Above, Neutra publicity emphasizes eradicating the boundary between indoors and out using the empty chairs.

1 Richard Neutra, *Trend Magazine*, October 1934.
2 *Fortune Magazine*, October 1935.

Opposite page, top:
Western face of classrooms
Neutra planted trees at the west edge of his cherished "outdoor classrooms."

Opposite page, bottom:
Plan

1934–1935 ‣ Beard House
1981 Meadowbrook Road, Altadena, California

Welder on construction site

Melba and William Beard were an aviatrix and an engineering professor whose parents, the radical Oxford-educated historian/activists Charles and Mary Beard, were close friends and admirers of the Neutras.

Despite making Neutra famous, the Lovell Health House, completed just as the 1929 stock market crashed, proved exorbitantly expensive. Although novel because of its steel framing, its equation of frame + cladding = wall was ancient. In July 1934, at the height of the Great Depression, Neutra turned to a new system that seemed far better suited to low-cost prefabricated housing: cheaper, easier to build and stronger, with cladding, load-bearing, heating and cooling all in one package. As a prototype, the 1,200-sq.-ft., $4,950 Beard House is virtually hand-crafted, down to the catches for the sliding windows and the unique sizes of each of the "commercial" sliding steel-and-glass doors.

In characteristic Neutra fashion, he compared the two systems with biological phenomena. He wrote, "The organic structural pattern of the inner skeleton, as with amphibians, reptiles and mammals [the Lovell House, the "mammal," with a Gunite skin], brought me to get interested also in the contrary successes of nature, the exoskeleton of the beetle [the Beard House, the beetle with its breathable but hard shell]." This special "shell" was devised not by world-famous architects like Adler and Sullivan (whose Chicago work inspired the Lovells' structure) but by a local man, architect/contractor Vincent Palmer, who welded steel panels to corrugated steel H. H. Robertson roof decking. Neutra later explained at a U.S. Navy symposium that the sheet metal sections "were meant to play their role as floor decks, but I used them with other enthusiastic collaborators as wall sections, quickly assembled and fitted [welded] together with their ceilings [either the same decking or open web steel joists for areas where spans were longer]. As this was a hollow section, I pushed up electrically hot air . . . to heat the interior space from all sides." The radiantly heated floor, with its air plenum sandwiched between a 12"-deep double-shell of diatomaceous earth, was to act like one monolithic heat panel like a modernized "ancient Roman bath," he wrote. The exterior openings at the base and top of the corrugated steel sandwiches, Neutra believed logically but erroneously, could also be harnessed to "inhale" cool air in the summer and "exhale" it at the top through small vents—thus mimicking the beetle's shell. (The cooling system never functioned, perhaps because the vents were too few or too small. The vents let rain in, too, Mary Beard said, though the radiantly heated floors still work.)

By vertically embedding the panels 16" into concrete footings to create stiffly cantilevered walls "designed to take lateral stresses such as wind attacks or earth shocks," the welded rigid house could withstand all but the most devastating earthquakes. Sited just below the scrubby San Gabriel Mountains, notorious for sudden, swift-moving fires, the all-steel home was also fire- and termite-resistant, a client requisite.

Other experimental measures were more successful. Special glass reduced solar gain. Neutra introduced what is probably the application of commercial ball-bearing

Plan

Opposite page:
View from the southeast

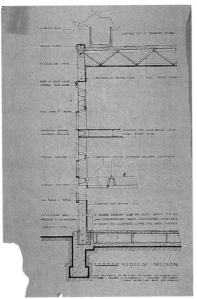

sliding glass-and-steel doors in an American home (now a residential default, though similar precedents include the sliding wood panels in Rudolph Schindler's 1922 home and the *shoji* screens Neutra admired on his 1930 trip to Japan) to connect the west and north walls to the gardens beyond. Thick vertical Palmer sections separating the glass are sheathed with shiny cadmium in a smooth parabolic shape recalling a 1930s car fender or airplane wing; the curve was also intended to "dematerialize" the wall by making the eye slide past the vertical interruption.

The 8' tall doors and 9' high ceilings, common in Neutra's 1930s houses, expand the sense of spatial largesse. The stainless steel-faced fireplace with its asymmetrically located firebox is positioned opposite the view; built-in seating facing the west garden creates a cozy inglenook. As usual, Neutra placed tall windows on the north sink wall of the kitchen with a "full mountain view for the benefit of the housewife" and installed a 12' white rubber countertop/drainboard, an innovation that cracked and discolored with time.

Many treatments beside radiant heating became Neutra trademarks. He often required elements to do "double duty." Here the entry lamps illuminate both sides of the entry. Exterior light strips in the roof overhang soften the transition between indoors and outdoors at night; doors were framed without case molding so that they became invisible in the wall plane. Large tempered Masonite panels, a cheap material, were wax-rubbed to glow a rich dark blond. Echoing traditional Japanese dwellings, a

North rear elevation

A third bedroom was attached to the northern wing in 1947. Neutra had designed a free-standing addition but Melba wanted the bedroom to be physically connected so that the parents were not separated from their children. Neutra refused to alter his commission, accepted a small fee and departed.

white plaster band runs above the 8' tall panels to unify the room. The house is relatively closed off to the street and open to nature in the rear, another typical Neutra solution in suburban houses.

When the house won a 1934 Gold Medal Award in the prestigious competition sponsored by Better Homes in America, a movement chaired by then-President Herbert Hoover to promote home ownership, Neutra must have felt that popular acceptance of systems building was very close. He did in fact use Palmer's system again for two other projects, the California Military Academy, 1935, and the lavish Josef von Sternberg House, 1936, as though probing the system's generic viability.

In a letter of 1981 to the Beard House's then new owner, Melba Beard wrote, "I regret that in our declining years, we do not now have a place like our Altadena house; it gave a freedom of spirit, a closeness to nature, a calm living. . . . which is the way Neutra meant it to be."

Opposite page, top:
Neutra stands at north-facing wall in what would become the eating area.

Opposite page, bottom:
Section of steel wall

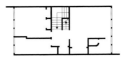 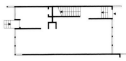

1937 ▸ Landfair Apartments
Landfair Avenue at Ophir Drive, Westwood, California

Street facade

Now virtually unrecognizable in its current guise as student housing, Landfair's allegiance to the Neue Sachlichkeit, "new objectivity," is unmistakable. With its recurrent stucco bands, razor-sharp rectangular volumes and ribbon windows, it resembled a displaced fragment of the experimental European Siedlungen, government-supported multi-family housing. (Neutra designed one model house in 1932 for the Werkbundsiedlung in Vienna.) In contrast, Landfair was very American in its private financing.

A staggered row of six two-bedroom flats, each 17' 10" x 36' 6", is sited on the west. On the east, two other, larger units pivot away from the rest of the composition, their porches facing away from the L-shaped composition for privacy and sun. Each unit included a balcony and a staircase leading to little rooftop penthouses alternating with wooden trellises. Neutra used internal clerestories to allow daylight to penetrate the middle of the units, where light would be dim. He also stacked the top-floor bathrooms above the kitchen, saving mechanical runs and enhancing privacy for those in the bedrooms. The 3' 3 1/2" module of his oft-used steel casement windows determined the width of each unit's step back into the site.

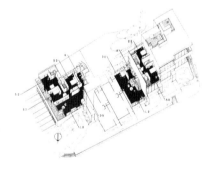

Cutaway

Opposite page, top:
Rear facade

Opposite page, bottom:
Plan of a two-story unit

1937 ▸ Miller House

2311 North Indian Avenue, Palm Springs, California

Opposite page:

Neutra used flagstone surrounded by grass to weave "die Wüste," the dessert, with the human-wrought orthogonal building.

The interiors of Neutra's best 1930s houses reveal his skill in layering spatial functions rather than treating them as distinct sequences. They share the elusive qualities of the light, thin Japanese tea house architecture he fell in love with at Katsura Imperial Villa on his 1930 world lecture tour. Nowhere is this influence more evident than in this 1,164-sq.-ft., $7,500 house, which improbably integrates a pueblo dwelling burrowed into the desert with a disciplined Modernism. The house became one of his most lauded achievements, not least because its result revealed the high quality of a resilient collaboration between architect and client.

Grace Lewis Miller was a sophisticated, middle-aged widow, an entrepreneur who transported the German "Mensendieck System of Functional Exercise" to the desert and then taught it to high-end clients when the city was raw and new. The technique involved a self-analysis of one's body moving in space to regain a wholesome posture and vitality, typically practicing moves nude in a mirror. All Neutra houses were to be therapeutic, but, like the Lovell Health House, here physical movement and the body formed the basis of the brief.

Miller knew she "didn't want a Rubens, she wanted a Picasso." While she considered Wright and even Philip Johnson, family lore says it was Neutra who arrived in a Packard with a trailer hitched to it, resplendent with pivoting drawing board and awning. (The pivot was to allow him to study sun and wind angles.) As the story goes, he would sit in the shade and sketch while his wife, Dione, played the cello in the sun.

The northeast corner is its "pueblo" side, its white stuccoed sides stepping back like traditional native architecture. The southeast corner also steps back, but here in clear glass, sliding out of its protective shell to reveal a roofed reflecting pool next to the screened porch. Miller was very pleased. "Water tempers the effect of the sunshine and sometimes makes beautiful reflections that dance on the ceiling of the living room and porch," she wrote in 1938. On the north side, large translucent glass with clerestories for cross-ventilation served to illuminate the moving body while conferring privacy upon it. (From his study of wind angles, on this side Neutra restricted openings because of the harsh, sand-carrying wind.) Mirrors at right angles to this wall effectively "doubled" the space devoted to the slow, deliberate movements his client taught. High built-in cabinetry, partly shielding her bed, separates this area from the rest of the studio/house; a curtain could be drawn across the room to give her complete visual privacy.

Just as Neutra layered spatial transitions, he also layered functions. As he once said, more optimistically than realistically, " . . . In our house rooms have no names such as living room, dining room, bedroom. . . . Rooms are portions of our great living space and pragmatically elastic." This "great living space" sounds very much like the Japanese concept of the *zashiki*, or flexible principal room, used for living, sleeping and entertaining, as in Miller's home.

Every detail deftly responded to a specific client. For example, near her "day or night couch," where she desired an unobstructed view of the reflecting pond and the horizon

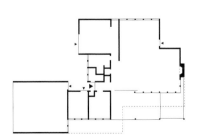

Plan

beyond, he pushed the casement windows up to the ceiling, so no vertical line would impede her gaze. Next to her closet, Neutra designed an alcove, tiny but flooded with north sunlight with translucent glass for her morning toilette. Here her makeup sat on a floating plane of veined ivory onyx, which gently illuminated her skin. The wardrobe is a portrait of Miller: it is her own personal machine for living. Its full-height cabinetry contains seven separate drawers, each a slightly different depth for each category of apparel. "How many sweaters do you own? How many hats?" Neutra wanted to know.

Neutra incorporated many strategies to enhance serenity. Miller's bedroom contains a pair of French doors, 3' 3" each. An exterior screen in the same overall dimension stood the same distance from the wall. To create a tiny porch, the doors could be

The curtain on the track permitted privacy in either studio, north, or living room, south. This is one of Neutra's most "Japanese interiors" in its strong datum lines, the white "folded" ceiling plane meeting the dark walls and in the flexibility and simplicity of its space.

secured with bolts at their base so that, held at right angles to the wall, they completed a rectangle. Thus, when she retired for the night she could enjoy the fragrant scent from the citrus trees planted beyond the porch. Olfactory sensuality was not confined to the bedroom. To the right of the kitchen sink, a flat aluminum panel opened. Trash could be disposed discreetly, and the receptacle emptied only from outdoors. Inside, Douglas fir plywood walls stained with a silver wash neutralized the aggressive sun.

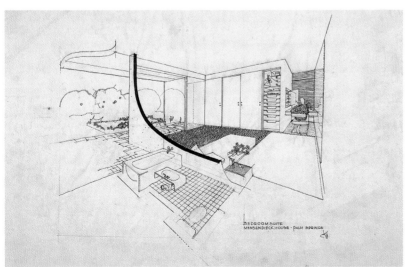

Mrs. Miller sits on the southeast screened porch; the reflecting pool created a micro-climate.

Cutaway rendering shows north end of Miller's onyx-topped dressing table, customized closets and private bedroom patio in the west.

1941–1942 ▸ Channel Heights Community
Western Avenue and 25th Street, San Pedro, California

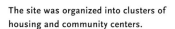
The site was organized into clusters of housing and community centers.

Overlooking the harbor of San Pedro in southern California, this now-demolished multi-unit project was exceptional in its careful planning for people and cars and in how it resolved dwelling on a spectacular but difficult site. Built for World War II shipbuilders, Channel Heights was the last permanent housing funded by the Federal Works Agency after the war began. It was built quickly, breaking ground in June 1942 and dedicated November 15 that year. The progressive community was racially integrated, something that was highly unusual before a 1948 US Supreme Court decision did away with "restrictive covenants." Sold after the war, the complex thrived for four more decades.

Neutra preserved the rugged character of the landscape by following the topography of the 150-acre property, consisting of one ravine dropping a dramatic 240' and several smaller canyons. Records indicate he designed 540 units in 222 buildings (60 one-bedroom, 378 two-bedroom and 162 three-bedroom units) as one- and two-story duplexes and four-plexes at a cost of between $2,600 and $4,400 per unit, according to conflicting contemporary sources, which also mentioned unit totals up to 600. As with the Nesbitt House, steel and aluminum (the war's "critical materials") were avoided in lieu of exteriors of redwood and plaster. Interior stucco walls and exposed roof insulation, placed above open-beam ceilings, were painted in soft pastels. Plastic, pot metal and cast iron served plumbing and mechanical systems. Neutra kept careful track of every cubic foot of material; he even designed the metal baffles for air supply ceiling outlets with his customarily disciplined lines.

He gave primacy to the pedestrian and fast-moving, hard-working wartime parent/resident in several ways using his signature "fingerpark" design based on the failed 1938 "Park Living" project in Florida. At Channel Heights, Neutra grouped the buildings into four areas separated by the ravines. Illuminated underpasses under high road embankments functioned as both surface drains and as "pedestrian communication," as he called it, between residential areas and the community buildings. Visitors entered through trellised pergolas onto park walks leading to the houses, which had park addresses rather than street numbers. Each of the diagonally oriented houses faced the park on one side and the ocean on the other. Driving and parking were relegated to service courts on cul-de-sacs.

Opposite page:
Neutra preserved as much of the original rolling hills of the site as possible.

With their contrasting panels of dark wood-siding and stair rails against the white walls, the small shed-roof houses conveyed a Japanese rusticity. Neutra energized their plain facades by breaking up the vertically grained redwood into two planes in which the middle section of the redwood steps out to house a roofed entry area for the units. For the interiors, he designed do-it-yourself furniture, such as the Boomerang Chair, an instant hit, first published in *Popular Mechanics*, as well as an egg-shaped coffee table. He also provided each unit, ranging from 394 to 820 sq. ft., with a balcony, accordion-style room dividers and plenty of storage space. Blank walls faced strong prevailing winds. Landscaping included "ample space for victory gardens and flowers," one brochure noted.

Cashier's office included surfaces of dark and light to make walls recede or step forward, as well as the globe lighting used throughout the project's public facilities.

    The all-redwood community structures included a school; a 40 x 72' social hall with sliding partitions and glass walls; workshops and play areas. He said that a cafeteria for the elementary school (portions of it curved and articulated like his early Ring Plan School) "should be included for the wartime effort and for future peace." The daycare center for school-aged children of working mothers was a necessity, he argued, adding that his plan "greatly facilitated the acquisition of wholesome toiletting habits of children" because additional bathrooms were placed next to outdoor play areas.

    The striking, high-ceilinged 9,000-sq.-ft. market (with its own nursery) on the west side of the complex featured an angled redwood roof and large, spread aluminum letters atop a long bank of tall glass windows.

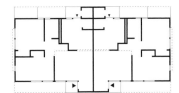

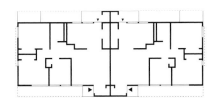

Unit plans

In the accelerated sweep of its facade, the community market recalls the 1921–23 addition to the *Berliner Tageblatt* building, which Neutra worked on under Eric Mendelsohn.

1941–1942 ▸ Nesbitt House

414 Avondale Avenue, Los Angeles, California

Rear elevation

Opposite page:
Street facade
In its simple materials, the brick and board-and batten exterior, left, recalls both American ranch houses and the Gothic Revival cladding for "cottages" espoused by 19th-century American tastemaker Andrew Jackson Browning.

Like Channel Heights, World War II's curtailment of "critical materials" provided an opportunity for Neutra to innovate. He called the 2,000-sq.-ft., $14,000 Nesbitt House the "war house" and "the last of an era" not only because of the wood throughout the house (Neutra had employed wood many times) but more importantly because of the techniques he was forced to use. Instead of steel casement windows housed in a machine aesthetic, the original house for Mr. and Mrs. John Nesbitt manifested a tactile, refined rusticity.

"It was built by elderly carpenters and masons on the premises who last year had not yet found their place at the running belt of new-fangled armament industries," he wrote for a 1945 issue of *Timber*, a magazine devoted to the Canadian wood industry. "This is not a lavishly finished, extravagant piece of jewelry or gadgetry that consumes the funds that should go into war bonds and war necessities. Life is reduced to simplicity . . . without domestic slaveys and gardeners . . ." Neutra locked the composition into the shady, secluded site through the palette of glass, redwood board and batten and Roman and common brick (used for low walls, the ground plane indoors and out and part of the two-box fireplace of shifting planes dividing living and study areas). Terminating the long angled pedestrian approach, a small pool at the entrance slipped under the glass walls, reinforcing the intimacy with the outdoors. (The angle also served to draw attention away from the garage attached to a separate building containing studio and bedroom, a kitchenette, fireplace and two bathrooms. Neutra

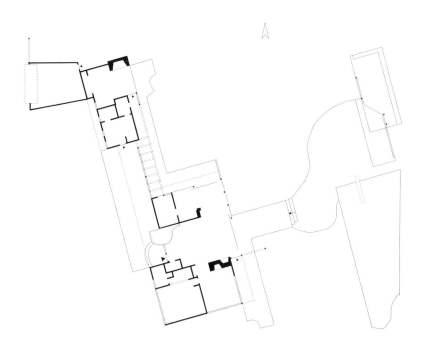

Plan

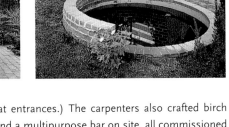

From left to right:

Master bedroom looking west; long brick approach to front door; the rounded, simple rustic ponds crafted from old brewery vats offset the orthogonality of the house.

always controlled views, especially at entrances.) The carpenters also crafted birch furniture, redwood built-ins, lamps and a multipurpose bar on site, all commissioned by the NBC radio producer and his wife. Old brewery vats cut into shallow sections 10' wide were sunk into the ground and bricked up on the outer edge to form a number of pools scattered throughout the grounds; the gesture offset the rectilinear volumes, as does the un-Neutraesque serpentine wall in the rear garden.

Despite the restricted palette, color wasn't eliminated. Between the beams in the studio the ceiling was yellow; some walls were blue-green, others Chinese red. Kitchen countertops were laid with eggplant linoleum top with light salmon accents. It was her favorite house, Dione Neutra said.

The composition is "locked" into the landscape: the entry pool integrates indoors
and outdoors and the walls of glass invite
immediate views of the backyard.

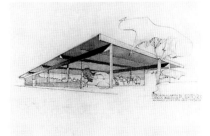

1944–1945 · Rural Health Centers
Puerto Rico

Opposite page, top:
Like Neutra's schools in the US, the classrooms Neutra designed opened on to the landscape.
Here, however, the material, concrete block and poured concrete, are crude and simple. The openings are devised from large commercial garage doors, which lift up instead of slide open.

Opposite page, bottom left:
An "escola urbana de 8 salas de aula," or eight-classroom urban school.
Classroom buildings flank outdoor individual "classroom patios" for upper grades. Outdoor assembly room, top of drawing, for lower grades.

Opposite page, bottom right:
The school for the industrial arts
included concrete-block supported acquariums and germinating beds. (From Neutra's *Architecture of Social Concern in Regions of Mild Climate*.)

The horizontal position of the doors, sometimes built without glass, facilitate ventilation.

Neutra's schools, rural health care centers, hospitals and community centers here are little known but rank among his best work. They were all part of a $50 million commission he received at the height of World War II, when many US architects' practices were languishing. The brief was no less than to employ architecture to eradicate the conditions that led to "miseria y hambre," misery and hunger. Neutra rejoiced in the challenge of designing cheap architecture with a restricted palette of materials, quickly assembled by unskilled labor, in addition to wisely acknowledging local traditions.

Like many Modernists who emerged from the 19th century, Neutra understood only too well the value of light and moving air and its impact on health. It was known that conquering tuberculosis owed more to 19th-century social reform movements than to the 1882 discovery of the tubercle bacillus or to treatment. Neutra's grandparents died in the mid-1850s from a typhoid epidemic; his father, Samuel, died in 1920 from the influenza then raging across Europe. Neutra himself almost died from malaria and apparent tuberculosis during his World War I military stint. It is no wonder, perhaps, that this personal history amplified his evolving concept of "biorealism," to the point that Neutra conceived good design as medicine for physical well-being.

He set up a site office in Puerto Rico in November 1943 and made six visits over the next 14 months, designing over 150 classrooms, over 120 rural health centers, nursing schools, housing and four hospitals with between 300 and 600 beds with "tubercular" wards, hydro and physiotherapy, radiation and labor rooms.

The strong horizontal character of all the buildings is enhanced by the stretches of metal "Miami" louvered blinds—one as much as 122' in length—and long masonry courses. In the medical facilities, narrow one-room-plus-corridor footprints were enhanced by openable windows, five-foot overhangs, breezeways and clerestories that ensured light, shade and a "continuous air exchange over lowered spandrels." Neutra also made his classrooms work hard: one whole wall of each 23 x 30' classroom module (conceived as additive units) pivoted up and out to double classroom size, to provide instant shade, draw the landscape in and obviate costly doors.

Neutra studied local social, economic, climatic and geographical conditions and described the "haunting night beauty" of the impoverished protectorate in letters to home. "Only through the psychological taking possession of [these] institutions by the entire community do they become appreciated communal property instead of just appearing to be the scheme of a distant government engaged in a showy drive against illiteracy and ill health," he wrote in his book *Architecture of Social Concern in Regions of Mild Climate*. Thus health centers were also designed as social places "where one plays dominoes in the evening, strums a guitar or dances on the spacious porch . . . a [concrete] bench around the wide opening of the milk dispensary is a stage for teachers or entertainers," he wrote. Rather than admonishing his clients about the evils of drink, he suggested having a café/bar near the inoculation centers to make having shots and blood tests more palatable.

1946–1947 ▸ Kaufmann House

470 West Vista de Chino, Palm Springs, California

A decade after Edgar Kaufmann, Sr., hired Frank Lloyd Wright to design the renowned Falling Water at Bear Run, he wanted to establish a West Coast base. Not impressed with Taleisin West—Wright's summer atelier hunkered into the Arizona bedrock—he turned to Richard Neutra, anticipating an equally brilliant voice but a lighter touch in Palm Springs, a town better known for frivolity than morality. (Unsurprisingly, Wright, who had once called Neutra's work "cheap and thin," was outraged.) Since the 1920s, the city at the foot of Mount San Jacinto drew Hollywood types seeking a getaway. Albert Frey, Le Corbusier's protégé, built his own house here in 1940; Neutra's tiny Miller House was completed in 1937, but the $348,000, 3,200-sq.-ft. Kaufmann House reigns today as a grand Modernist villa, a recently landed silver aircraft on a green carpet weighted down only by carefully positioned boulders on this "moonscape," as Neutra called it.

The "Wüstenlandschaft," or the desert, or more precisely, the wilderness around Palm Springs, fascinated Neutra. In his 1927 book *Wie baut Amerika* he concluded with images of pueblos in New Mexico and Arizona, praising their stacked rooms with rooftop terraces and the ability of mudbrick masses to respond to a punishing climate. Despite the polished precision of the Kaufmann House, it suggests the spirit of the pueblos he admired.

Though both Falling Water and the Kaufmann House share a use of stone masonry and a floating weightlessness, Neutra emphasized his architectural distance from Wright in that his buildings were "made, not grown." He "inserted" the house into this harsh backdrop. It was "set on footings," whose juxtaposition of artifice and artificial climate underscored "the weather, the silver-white moonlight, and the starry sky."

Like other seminal 1940s projects, here the volumes relax into the site without relinquishing the taut quality of his earlier work. The Kaufmann House distills space into silver horizontal planes sliding above transparent glass. The only pronounced vertical is the chimney flanking the "gloriette," as Neutra called it. This is the rooftop space that crowns the house, a man-made mountain peak with a hearth. (As with his own house, Neutra deftly evaded a second-story prohibition by eliminating the gloriette's walls except for the fireplace and the movable vertical aluminum louvers. Aesthetically, they define a diaphanous plane; functionally, they act as a wind shield. He also had the foundations dug and permits pulled just before a wartime building moratorium began.)

Neutra's original drawing of the pinwheel floorplan reveals other contrasts. Using loose curves, the landscaping percolates through the orthogonal design. In contrast, taut parallel lines drawn on the diagonal represent the high winds and sand storms so common at the northern end of Palm Springs. This move animates the drawing but also reflects reality: the winds from the northwest are relentless, blasting whatever they can carry into the house even today, despite the upgrades, louvers, and solid walls. (And though having so much unprotected glass on the dwelling's south side may seem perverse in the desert, the house was to be used for one month a year—January.)

Opposite page:
View from the southeast
Master bedroom to the right and beyond the pool. Bronze window screens softened the composition's silvery gleam.

Certainly Neutra's plan, an extrovert in the landscape, owes much to Wright. With the living area at the hub, the pinwheel ensures that the four spines of single-volume rooms get both daylight and cross-ventilation. However, the pinwheel's arms, terminating with bedrooms and patios, also reveal a specific social order. Hosts, servants, children and guests are granted "extreme" privacy. Their opportunities to mingle occur in shaded walkways, living areas and the outdoor patios. The louvers flanking the long, dark lily pond connect the guest wing to the rest of the house, creating a sand-protected and water-cooled patio.

Radiant heat extends to the pool area; Neutra even placed it in the low seating wall linking house and pool, a socially magnanimous gesture that ensures the party continues on a chilly winter's night for shivering wet bathers or formally dressed party-goers.

To enhance the design's famous floating quality, the structural system combines wood and steel in such a way that the number of requisite vertical supports (which are slender in any case) are minimized. This is most emphatic in the southeast living room, whose glass-and-steel walls slide away while the roof and the beam supporting the sliders stretch out, spatially linking the house and the pool. This "outrigger" detail

The "gloriette"

Top:
View from master bedroom to pool

The living-room wall and the aligned dining table define the airy walkway to the master suite, left, and the living area with Neutra's prototypical "spider leg," right.

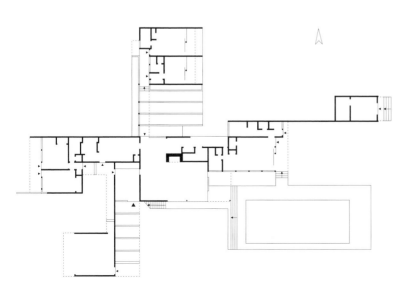

Plan
Strong desert winds come from the northwest, hence Neutra placed aluminum louvers connecting the guest wing, north, with the house as well as in the open gloriette on the second "floor."

became his best-known trademark: the spider leg, the umbilical cord fusing the landscape and the building.

A second strata of contrast is manifest in the materials: The light-colored, dry-set (mortared from behind) "Utah buff" stone Neutra used indoors and out creates a rich *chiaroscuro* effect, complementing the smoothness of the other finishes. However, even the stonework is carefully chiseled, both in the original—for which Neutra trained the masons who had worked on Falling Water, whom Kaufmann had flown in—and in the five-year restoration by the new owners in the mid-1990s.

One lively detail occurs at the southern gutters. At their eastern end, the fascias suddenly become much narrower just before they terminate, allowing any overflow rainwater to flow east beyond the building before it falls on rocks below, a feature seen

Above left:
The aluminum louvers and low pond connect house to guest suites. The profile of the design echoes Mt. San Jacinto in the distance.

Above right:
While the house opens up to the landscape in the rear, its ashlar facade shields the house from the street in good Adolf Loosian fashion.

in both Japanese gardens and medieval cathedrals. Banal gutters become Modernist gargoyles adept at romance. This indeed is a celebration of falling water, a long way from Bear Run.

1947–1948 · Tremaine House

1636 Moore Road, Montecito, California

Neutra wrote poignantly about the *genius loci* of this place in *Mysteries and Realities of the Site*. One immediately senses the majesty of this remote locale, with its gnarled oak trees, dappled light and the smell of the sea a few miles away. The sloping site is marked by carefully located "veins of enormous stone blocks like sculptures by Arp," Neutra wrote.

The house is reserved. Only the tips of its white beams beckon from the hushed road. That single beckoning comprises the street "facade." Moving closer, one's journey is then defied by the stone walls protecting the patio and the guest wing. It is one of many moments of tension rendered here in a poised equilibrium between floating and being anchored, solid and transparent, machine-made and nature-worn.

The union between architectural expression and structural system makes this house unique in Neutra's œuvre. Articulated concrete pillars bear the long frontal girders. Above them rests 7 x 16" cantilevered cross beams, which in turn support an impossibly thin 5" deep roof slab, all rendered in reinforced concrete in response to the threat of forest fires. Like Neutra's theoretical Diatom IV House of 1923 and his Puerto Rico classrooms of 1944–45, the system allows for both continual ventilation below the ceilings and ambient daylight; at night the light from inside illuminates the 'basso profondo' areas of the structure.

Where a younger Neutra accepted structural redundancy in a building system (e.g., the Palmer technique of load-bearing walls in the Beard House), the elder Neutra did not. Here the concrete pillars follow a 16' module only when needed. Where other concerns and load-bearing needs coincided, he exploited the latent plastic qualities of the grid and increased the pillar spacing to 20'. At the southeast corner of the living room, or "social quarters," as he called them, Neutra rendered one load-bearing member in stainless steel, not concrete, as a round column, not a rectangular pier. In good Neutra biorealistic fashion, this dematerialized the column so that the eye flows around it to connect spaces rather than to separate them.

In contrast to the crisp edges of the white of the beams and the roof slabs, Neutra used a rough native stone for walls. The terrazzo floors flow inside and out, radiantly heated even to the tip of the extravagant 56'-long west terrace, further serving to extinguish the indoor/outdoor boundaries. On the west side of the "social quarters" Neutra enlarged the living space by placing rotating walnut shade louvers at the edge of the overhang, which are operated by the touch of a toe pedal.

Like the Kaufmann House, the Tremaine House is also a pinwheel in plan. However even though the east and west arms are longer here, it is more socially centralized than its desert cousin. Whereas the Kaufmann House was built as a second home for one couple where privacy prevailed, the Tremaine House was designed for a family with three children. Contact was desirable. Inside, spaces merge into each other easily and have been designed to be reconfigured at will. Glass or wood (stained a "very dark purplish black") partitions slide. Neutra's "Camel" dining table lowers to coffee table height; the Neutra-designed sectional ottomans can be grouped together or dispersed.

Opposite page:
View from west terrace to family bedroom wing

Top:
View from terrace past dining patio to
bedroom wing in the north

Above:
Entrance walk

In the master bedroom the ground plane comes up almost to the window sill, so that nature is present in a muted morning light. (Neutra suggested that upon rising, the vista of an uninterrupted horizon was a bit too global in scope.) Below the house, an art gallery opens on to a "garden hall." Here again nature is both near and far: to the north lie ferns and shade, whereas the south opens on to a broad meadow, akin to the famously ill-kempt, happy meadow at the Eames House.

No other commission gave the architect more freedom in interior decoration and furniture design. The Neutra office specified rugs, drapes and bedspreads, accounting for fabric yardage, cost, manufacturers and color for the children's bedrooms, one in chartreuse, another in yellow, the third in salmon. Many off-the-shelf items were customized, such as the copper porch furniture, for which the manufacturer retooled his jigs to tighten tube radii and curves to give thinner and crisper profiles.

In 1954, Neutra wrote to Warren and "Kit" Tremaine, " Your house—in my mind— has been perhaps my greatest creative experience. . . . I do not believe that our pursuit of happiness, which is life, is just to find a comfortable situation. . . . The human physiology, the human mind and soul, is such that it must sing out its own epic story and crown it with some fragrant fulfillment and achievement . . . not everything, not even writing the Missa Solemnis or painting the Sistine Chapel, solves life and dissolves all its bitterness . . ."

Left:

Looking south into the "social quarters"

Below:

White concrete contrasting with rough flagstone walls of entrance carport

Plan

Like the Kaufmann House, this is also a "pinwheel," but with private areas less overtly separated, illuminating a different family structure.

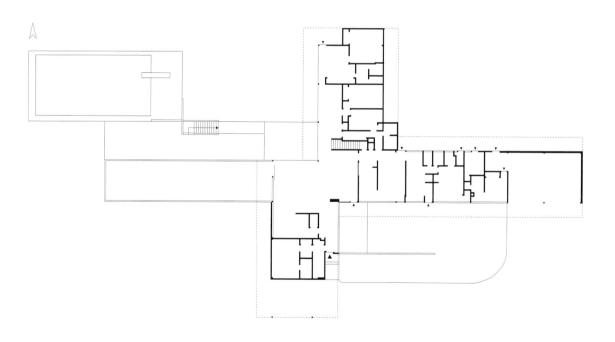

1946–1948 · Case Study House #20

219 Chautaugua Boulevard, Pacific Palisades, California

Opposite page:
Looking west to "social patio"

Right:
View from the south

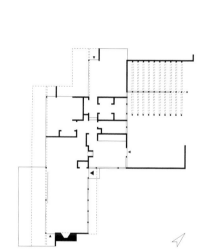

Plan
showing four outdoor areas as rooms for
entertaining, dining, playing and working.

This modest, award-winning house is known as Case Study House #20, and embodies
one of Neutra's most beloved strategies, the "Four-Courter House" scheme. A few
minutes' walk from the Charles and Ray Eames House, it is part of a Case Study House
"colony" of famous houses all sharing a five-acre meadow-and-woodland tract overlooking the Pacific Ocean. John Entenza, editor of *Arts and Architecture* magazine and
founder of the radical CSH program, owned the tract.

A quarter of a century earlier Neutra had conducted his own private "case study"
program, exploring alternatives to stick framing. While younger architects around him
now hotly pursued the potential of steel and glass—as he had with the Health House

Dale Bailey's bedroom became the south end of the new dining room with a fireplace suspended from the roof and surrounded by daylight.

"My wife and I thought weeks about it," Stuart Bailey said, "and Neutra took three minutes."

—Neutra's CSH houses were conventional post-and-beam, whose explorations were spatial, not structural.

Stuart Bailey, a 30-year-old dentist, bought his lot from Entenza for $9,000. For the new family man, part of the program's appeal was gifts and discounts from manufacturers such as three 12 x 8' sliding glass-and-steel doors and a prefabricated utility core called the Ingersoll that centrally massed plumbing and heating equipment that "still works fine after 55 years." The compact house (1,320 sq. ft. for $19,600 or $14.85 per sq. ft.) began as two offset redwood, white stucco and brick rectangles. To accommodate the future children, Neutra anticipated additions beginning with a freestanding two-bedroom unit connected by a walkway in 1950. Others followed in 1958 and 1962, adding 1,650 sq. ft. The home now sports four articulated wings jutting out into the landscape. The resulting outdoor "four courts" included social quarters, playing quarters, dining quarters and working quarters, essentially doubling its "square foot livability index," a favorite RJN measure.

Living room viewed from the southeast

Neutra regularly applied Gestalt theories to alter spatial perceptions, but young Bailey didn't know that when he innocently asked if the closet interiors could be painted white, to see things better. "Mr. Bailey," Neutra sternly replied, "the closets must recede. If you paint them white, I will remove my name from the project." (They remain dark brown.)

"The thing I like about this house," said Dr. Bailey recently, nodding to the trees beyond the glass walls, "is that there is no house."

1949·Wilkins House

528 Hermosa, South Pasadena, California

In architectural literature it has always been stated that Neutra's Case Study House #6, Omega, and #13, Alpha (featured in the March 1946 issue of *Arts and Architecture*), designed as a pair on adjacent lots, remained unbuilt. Neutra named his hypothetical Mr. and Mrs. Alpha (clients for #13) and Mr. and Mrs. Omega (clients for #6) to show his architecture fit humanity from A to Z, though the couples were white suburban Americans.

It is now likely that Neutra "lifted" the Alpha design and applied it to a real client on a real lot. The drawings for #13, a one-story, L-shaped house, were as complete as for any real client, down to the tangent of the peephole for the front door, drawn at full scale. A generous flagstone breezeway at right angles to the entrance path and cutting through the building separates the two arms of the L; the big gesture runs out beyond both sides of the house, creating two separate but linked angled terraces, another variation on Neutra's "Four-Court" idea. The fireplace with its two fireboxes, one indoor, one for outdoor entertaining, acts as the hub of the plan.

Mrs. Alpha requested that it be laid in flagstone because "on the occasion of picnic parties, with youngsters about, there would probably be continuous traffic from one open air terrace to the other—root beer to be spilled and greasy sandwiches to drip." Coincidentally, a Mrs. George Wilkins—a real client who with her husband purchased a quiet, wooded double lot in South Pasadena in late 1947—had the exact same concerns about root beer and greasy sandwiches. And like Mrs. Alpha, it was her "specific wish" that there be a "psychological connection" between the two terraces (pure Neutra-speak, who also referred to her kitchen as a "culinary production center"). So Neutra designed identical breezeways for both women. In fact, portions of the client descriptions for real or hypothetical client match word for word, just as the plans agree almost line for line. One length of a building wall was 22' 11", the other plan called out the same wall at 22' 9". The idiosyncratic angles on the terrace overhangs match.

The detailing of the house included a little-seen but elegant ventilation strategy in the living room and master bedroom, with screened birch panels placed below a row of casement windows. Hinged from the top, they introduced air inside when curtains were drawn. It also allowed the casements to be without screens, which Neutra avoided where possible because they compromised the outdoor view.

Living room viewed from the southwest

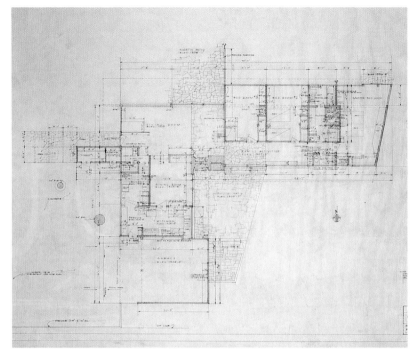

Left:

Case Study House "Alpha" plan
Virtually identical to the Wilkins House plan

Below left:

Redrawn plan for house on right can apply either to the Wilkins or Alpha House. The left plan is Neutra's proposed, unbuilt house for the parents of the Wilkins. Despite its "harmonious relationship," as he wrote to the Wilkins, the boxy plan for the real parents is not that of the Alpha's original partner, the Omega Case Study House. The Omega was in the cross-shaped, "four-court" style à la Case Study House #20.

Below Right:

Neutra disliked window screens because they physically and aesthetically compromised the seamless—and necessary—experience he sought for the user, one that blended indoors and out. Here his clever but rarely employed ventilating screens on the living room's south wall, now restored, permit cross-breezes when open and is disguised as conventional wall paneling when closed.

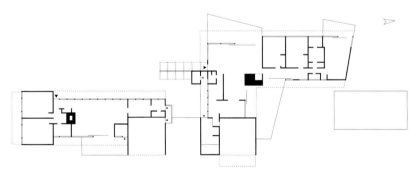

Living room viewed from the north

East living room wall

1951 ‣ Hinds House

3940 San Raphael Avenue, Los Angeles, California

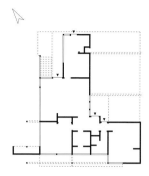

Above:
Plan

Right:
West facade

View of northwest corner

Neutra reduced the view facade of this L-shaped, 1,240-sq.-ft. house to one plane consisting of wood, glass and stucco. This plane continues beyond the building envelope to frame a terrace on the north. Below, a tall, narrow storage shed flanked by two parallel spider legs delicately anchors the house to the hill.

Jay and Catharine Hinds had never heard of Neutra but saw his work in *If You Want to Build A House*, published by the Museum of Modern Art, New York, in 1946, promoting small, postwar, modern designs to solve the housing shortage. A year after the house was built they wrote to thank him for helping them choose a site, remarking on "the majestic view and feeling of spaciousness in our really small house. We somehow blindly stumbled into your office, and now are even more amazed that you accepted our modest commission . . ."

Opposite page:
Master bedroom viewed from the southwest

1953·Auerbacher House
121 Sierra Vista Drive, Redlands, California

Opposite page:
Looking southeast from playroom/solarium along the building's north face

Right:
The ashlar fireplace's deliberate asymmetry was a classic Neutra imperative.

Far right:
Master bedroom viewed from the southeast

Plan

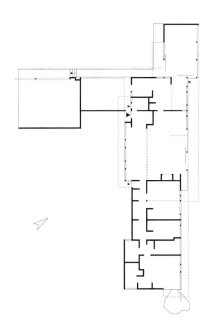

The 2,300-sq.-ft. house commissioned by Frederick and Mary Jane Auerbacher sits above orange layers of suburban sprawl and below the grade of a winding street. One wall of this narrow box is almost a continuous plane of glass facing a mountain range while the reclusive street side is closed except for clerestories. Some internal walls running at right angles to this long rectangle appear not to touch the "view" wall because floor-to-ceiling glass is used for the last two feet of these short walls. The gesture animates an interior visual corridor, confers a sense of transparency throughout the house, and demonstrates Neutra's idea on the role of peripheral vision in accessing nature.

While the house is thus aesthetically bisected longitudinally, it is laterally bisected functionally. A carefully orchestrated spine of rooms is terminated by a tranquil master bedroom at the east end of the house, where a mitered glass corner leads the eye out to a corner pool and intimate landscaping (as at the Tremaine House, Neutra typically exploited nearby greenery for bedrooms and horizons for public areas). At the west end lies a sturdy, light-filled work and play room off the kitchen, where the sink played "central command post" for watching children in any area. While the bedrooms are painted in flat whites, dark browns and greens, the living and dining area combine birch paneling, redwood tongue-and-groove ceiling and a flagstone fireplace. (Mary Jane Auerbacher said that Neutra admonished the stonemason, who had also built the fireplace at the Neutra-designed Auerbacher Lodge, 1952, to be sure to lay the stone so that none commanded a center position or achieved symmetry.) Neutra also provided a "music nook" in the living area for her, a professional musician, that is attuned to every possible need for sheet music and instrument storage. Here the room juts out with a full height, short glass wall, again providing a slice of dark, "near greenery." Neutra designed all the furniture; for two prominent living-room chairs, he added side wood pieces to cover the cross-braced diagonal, which he hated. To make other furniture appear to float, he made their legs as thin as possible. In the dining area, Neutra placed a low mirror behind the dining room table (aligned along the window wall) so that all guests could enjoy the mountain view.

1953·Eagle Rock Park Clubhouse

1100 Eagle Vista Drive, Los Angeles, California

This building, essentially a pavilion open on three sides, ranks as one of Richard and Dion Neutra's finest works. This minimalist pavilion, light steel frame clad in stucco and brick, stands in a large public park and has continually been used, for proms and plays, as a meeting hall and athletic venue. It is also a finely proportioned composition in asymmetry, whose broad horizontal planes and overhangs contrast with the precise rhythm of thin steel columns that sometimes function as spider legs. The exceptionally deep overhangs are a delight for children playing underneath them in rain or sun.

Three sides open at will, which fosters its enduring flexibility for different uses. The main hall has wide lift-up doors on the east and west ends, encouraging activities to flow between indoors and out and emphasizing a light shelter with minimal structural intrusion. To support the large east overhang, Neutra employed the same strategy as he did for the Health House balconies, by suspending the overhang's roof beams with slender steel hangars from the cantilevered beams of the tall main hall. Dion Neutra pointed out that the columns "supporting" the deep porch were placed there later by employees who, believing the cantilever would fail, inserted the clumsily steel columns.

On the north side, a stage opens up either to the main hall or to an outdoor amphitheater set into a shallow hill. The amphitheater beyond is separated from the stage by

From left to right:

Reflecting pool, later filled in, in north; looking north along the east facade; looking east along the north wall.

a pool and landscaping designed by Garrett Eckbo; this has a sense of permeable enclosure created by walls that are set increasingly further apart the further they extend up the hillside, integrating the clubhouse and the hill.

The clubhouse manifests Neutra's gift for creating architecture not as an arbiter of human behavior but as a neutral canvas primed for human endeavor.

Opposite page:

East facade

1964 · Taylor House

3816 Lackerbie Court, Glendale, California

"Floating fireplace" on the living room's south wall

The narrow rectangle on a strip of a site lies on "a really unapproachable piece of land at the end of a dead-end street," Neutra wrote. The small house is spacious, organized, easy-going. No attitude. The dwelling stands above fairly dense suburbia, and yet once inside, privacy and stunning up-close views of the oak trees as well as the panorama of the San Fernando Valley confer instant serenity. Maurice and Marceil Taylor's children were grown and gone when the couple commissioned the house. This was their pied-à-terre.

Neutra's standard repertoire of spatial relationships can be witnessed in this little house, although they are compressed, as if saying that a concisely rendered small stroke works just as well as a grand gesture. In plan, the private path starts from the carport in the northwest, leads to the kitchen and opens out to either an outdoor terrace on the northeast, to the dining/sitting area or through an opening to the "book" end of the living room. It continues to flow diagonally past this central space with its east floor-to-ceiling glass wall. The transition to the master suite begins with the fireplace. Here the path forks, either to the smaller bedroom and bath in the southwest or to the master bedroom at the southeast corner. In classic Neutra language, the fireplace is pulled away from the window wall and placed at right angles to it. By cantilevering it and enlarging the hearth, Neutra imbued it with a sense of weightlessness; by using both Roman and common red brick around a plaster firebox, he added texture. Beyond the fireplace, the core of bathrooms, floor-to-ceiling cabinetry and the dressing area create privacy for the master suite. There are few doors, which have been supplanted by full-height mahogany built-in cabinetry throughout the entire house.

Other small features occur at the front door (Neutra typically separated public and private access, which usually connected to the kitchen), where a simple, dark burlap panel compresses space and prolongs the delay in seeing the entire living room's wall of glass and, typically, a squirrel or two darting along the gray oak branches beyond. The master bath adds a special feature, giving it the feel of a rustic Japanese spa. Here one glass wall next to the sunken bathtub invites one to rub noses with a coyote or deer drifting by.

Opposite page:
North facade

Plan
A line of oak trees runs along east glass wall.

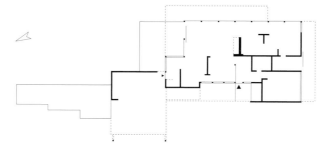

1965–1966·VDL Research House II

2300 E. Silverlake Boulevard, Los Angeles, California

Opposite page:
View southwest across the reflecting pool, which was meant to "merge" visually with Silverlake in the background.

The loss of the first VDL building, with its decades of drawings and client records, devastated the Neutras . . . and then they rebuilt it. The phoenix, VDL II, is more complex than its predecessor, more varied in section and has fewer "soft" materials. Though more transparent, it is also more introverted, addressing the internal garden more than the passerby on the boulevard. It plays more tricks of spatial illusion, and the addition of balconies makes the second design feel more like a tree house than a townhouse. Los Angeles had grown. Neutra's nemesis, "rolling traffic," and its accompanying pollution, now lay just beyond the front door. After the fire there were no buffers to shield the house from the strong western sun. The reservoir had been downsized so that its cooling presence stood 600' away. Two-story, electronically controlled aluminum "airplane" louvers rise from a curving pool at the entrance, providing immediate relief from the strong afternoon sun. The office and practice moved to the nearby Glendale office. Dion designed much of the new building while the Neutras traveled in Europe, Richard editing the work from abroad.

Once again, the Neutras adroitly sidestepped building codes, arguing that since the guesthouse and middle portion survived, more than 50 percent of the house remained, meaning they could use the existing footprint and floor joists.

The new design included a generous office, aligned with the guesthouse and separated from it by a carport. Inside the main house, a glass wall flanking an open-tread staircase replaced the solid walls of the original interior staircase. A 10'-wide, screened window near the upstairs breakfast nook slides entirely outside the building, bringing

Street facade

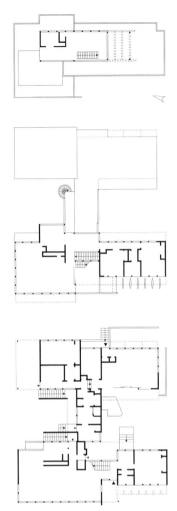

trees and sky into the interior, Dion's response to Dione's request to have an old-fashioned, screened-in porch. The kitchen was cantilevered three feet out to the rear. Glass walls rise above the built-in birch cabinets, which push out beyond the building envelope so the cabinetry doesn't decrease daylight at the countertop and to "surround the housewife" with foliage. Folding panels above countertop height encouraged a greater connection between the kitchen and the living room. Maintenance-free Formica paneling in a rosewood pattern replaced the original Masonite. Gold heat-reflecting privacy glass, now fixed, was used for the bed- and bathroom windows on the street facade. Inside, multiple mirrors above head height not only stretch space but sometimes also disorient the viewer.

The presence of water was a precious component in biorealism. Since the lake was now a distant sliver of silver, water was now integrated into each of the three stories. On the second floor, a pool was added to the outdoor patio (now bereft of its languid leather couches). An open-tread diagonal stair leads to the new, larger penthouse, where glass and steel replaced the original wood framing. Nautical-looking, curved sheet metal hiding roof mechanical equipment gives the new facade a very different look than its predecessor's from the street. Two inches of water surrounding the penthouse creates a microclimate while enabling the beholder to enjoy the mountain and lake view from the low redwood deck; the water also incidentally serves to insulate the house below. The perimeter seating of the little volume is deliberately low, so that when sitting and looking at the lake, the two water surfaces fuse into one silver sea.

Left:
View north from living room

Right:
Plans
Top, penthouse; middle, upper floor; bottom, ground floor showing connection to guesthouse

Opposite page:
Looking from the south bedroom "through" the kitchen

1966 · Bucerius House
Navegna, Switzerland

Neutra's best European houses have a different character from their American counterparts. Their level of finish is very high, and they feature luxurious materials, such as brushed stainless steel, walnut and marble. The wood used for the ceilings shows a thinner, more polished profile. And while some of his US homes enjoy extraordinary desert backdrops offsetting his taut lines and planes, many more are the instantly recognizable exceptions in conventional suburbanscapes. While the "nature" around them may indeed be "necessary for survival," it is a nature domesticated, tame and predictable.

In contrast, the commissions—and their handsome budgets—for the Bucerius, Pescher, Rang, Rentsch, and Tuia houses of the 1960s afforded Neutra the means to

The penthouse view
Looking southwest over Lago Maggiore

express with extraordinary means a relationship with a "nature" far less benign and altogether unpredictable, that of the Swiss Alps.

The imposing three-story east-west oriented house perches on a steep mountainside and overlooks Lago Maggiore, 2,000' below, a long lake set amidst a countryside of stunning beauty, where improbable subtropical plants, such as date palms and purple bougainvillea, thrive in the Swiss Alps. Directly below is the medieval town of Ascona, vacation draw for anarchists Bakunin and Kropotkin and early devotees of psychoanalysis and modern dance. Gerd Bucerius, famed as an intellectual, a progressive politician and the founder of *Die Zeit* newspaper, commissioned Neutra to design the house ($4 million Swiss francs then, or about $550,000), which quickly

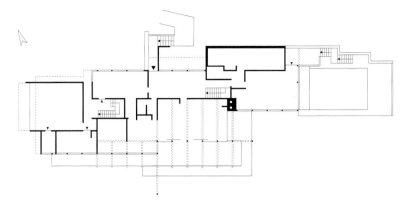

Middle level plan

Stairs under construction

gained cachet as a superb party venue. When Gerd and his wife separated, it became "Casa Ebelin" with a décor of chintz and coverings decidedly different in character from her husband's and Neutra's tastes.

Once at the house, one partakes of the mountain panorama only by traversing the large east-west entry hall. On the south side, Neutra articulated the library, dining and living rooms not with walls but by stepping each space back sequentially into the hill and away from the huge sweep afforded by the long glass wall, so that the "social area" lies at the heart of the house.

Neutra terminated the master suite, as well as the south and east end of the living room, with "waterguards," as he called them: shallow, linear strips of water at terrace edges that reflect the ever-changing sky. As at the Rentsch House, these strips are flanked on the lakeside by flat-lying railings of steel cables, so that nothing obstructs the view or, for that matter, provides any degree of psychological security vis-à-vis the precipice.

On the ground floor, Neutra's most extraordinary pool occurs, reminiscent of the pool at the Lovell Health House in intention if far more sophisticated in execution. The larger portion of the pool is open to the mountains, the other angles indoors under the house to the human artifice of smoothly honed stone walls wrapping around a "winter garden." Large movable glass partitions, both above and below the surface of the water, seal off the heated interior portion of the pool with the flick of a switch.

On the top floor, Neutra established yet another ground plane, here with a European "gloriette" surrounded by an elongated pool. A rooftop dumbwaiter affords opportunities for oblations to accompany the contemplation of one's place in the universe.

Opposite page:
View from the southwest

Life and Work

1892 ▶ Born April 8 in Vienna, Austria.

1910 ▶ Reads Friedrich Nietzsche and Rainer Maria Rilke. Develops lifelong friendship with Ernst Freud—son of Sigmund—who becomes an architect.

1911–1915, 1917–1918 ▶ Studies architecture at the Technical University, Vienna, where he is influenced by Otto Wagner and Adolf Loos. In his second year, he enters Loos's studio/salon. His studies include six years of Greek and eight years of Latin. He graduates in 1918 *summa cum laude*.

1914 ▶ Discovers Frank Lloyd Wright's Wasmuth *Folios*, published in 1910/11.

1914–1917 ▶ Neutra becomes Artillery Officer in the Imperial Austrian Army in Albania and Serbia. Reads writings of Wilhelm Wundt and Gustav Fechner—founders of experimental psychology—in which they expound upon their theories of the perception of space, sense perception and quantitative research.

1919 ▶ Recuperates from malaria and apparent symptoms of tuberculosis at convalescent home in Stäfa near Zurich. Meets Alfred and Lilly Niedermann, and their 18-year-old daughter and Richard's future wife, Dione. Works for Gustav Ammann, a landscape architect, at Otto Froebel's Erben landscaping company-cum-nursery, where he learns about plants, trees and site planning.

1920 ▶ In July, in a letter to Dione, Neutra writes, "A well-designed house affects our entire sense of space . . . a sense of smell, of touch, of hearing, of temperature and the eye . . . also an obscure sense of materials."

1921 ▶ Appointed city architect of Luckenwalde, Germany. Conceives a master plan of the city, which includes the landscaping.

1921–1923 ▶ Hired as assistant architect by Eric Mendelsohn in Berlin. Works on the Mossehaus, the headquarters of the *Berliner Tageblatt*.

1922 ▶ Marries Dione Niedermann, with whom

Richard and Dione Neutra

he has three children: Frank, 1924; Dion, 1926; and Raymond, 1939.

1923 ▶ Emigrates to the United States, where he works as a draftsman at C. W. Short and Maurice Courland, New York.

1924 ▶ February, employed as draftsman #208 at Holabird and Roche, Chicago. Initially lives at Hull House, where he meets Jane Adams, a social activist. Visits the work of Wright and Sullivan. Meets Wright at Sullivan's funeral. Dione joins Richard in June. In July, the couple arrives at Wright's Taliesin East in Wisconsin, where Richard is promised $160/month plus board.

1925 ▶ In February the couple moves to Los Angeles, where they rent an apartment in Rudolph and Pauline Schindler's North Kings Road House. Neutra works with Schindler on Wright's and independent projects. Begins Rush City Reformed, a visionary metropolis. Starts private practice.

1925–1950
Diatom Series

1927 ▶ Neutra and Schindler take part in the League of Nations competition in Geneva. They jointly found the "Group of Industry and Commerce," which designs the Jardinette Apartments, Los Angeles. Publishes *Wie baut Amerika* (How Does America Build).
Lovell Physical Culture Center, Los Angeles, CA

1929 ▶ American representative at the Congrès Internationaux d'Architecture Moderne (CIAM) in Brussels.
Lovell Health House, Los Angeles, CA

1930 ▶ Global tour starting in Japan in June, where he visits modern buildings and the Katsura Imperial Villa with architect Kameki Tsuchiura, whom he met at Taliesin East. Lectures in Berlin in the fall at the Metal Workers' Union designed by Erich Mendelsohn. At the invitation of Ludwig Mies van der Rohe, becomes visiting professor at the Bauhaus, Dessau. Introduced to Lyonel Feininger, Paul Klee and Gestalt theorists. Meets future benefactor Cornelius van der Leeuw. Stays at Gerrit Rietveld's Schröder House, Utrecht, Holland.

1931 ▶ Rents bungalow on Douglas Street, Echo Park, California. Student apprentices include Gregory Ain, Harwell Hamilton Harris and Raphael Soriano.

1932 ▶ The only West Coast architect to participate in the "Modern Architecture" exhibition at the Museum of Modern Art, New York, where his work is featured with that of Mies van der Rohe, Jacobus Oud, Walter Gropius, Le Corbusier, among others.
Exhibition House in Vienna, Austria
Van der Leeuw Research House, Los Angeles, CA

1933
Koblick House, Atherton, CA
Mosk House, Hollywood, CA
Universal-International Building, Hollywood, CA

1934 ▶ Beard House wins Gold Medal of the "Better Homes in America" competition cosponsored by the *Architectural Forum*. Mosk House and Koblick House win honorable mention; all

three lauded as "examples of a serious and in-formed effort to solve the problem of American life."
Scheyer House, Los Angeles, CA
Sten and Frenke House, Santa Monica, CA

1935
Beard House, Altadena, CA
California Military Academy, Culver City, CA
Corona School, Bell, CA
Largent House, San Francisco, CA

1936
Douglas Fir Plywood House, Westwood, CA
Kun House #1, Los Angeles, CA
Richter House, Pasadena, CA
Von Sternberg House, Northridge, CA

1937
Aquino Duplex, San Francisco, CA
Barsha House, North Hollywood, CA
Darling House, San Francisco, CA
Davis House, Bakersfield, CA
Hofmann House, Hillsborough, CA
Kaufman House, Westwood, CA
Kraigher House #1, Brownsville, TX
Landfair Apartments, Westwood, CA
Malcolmson House, Los Angeles, CA
Miller House, Palm Springs, CA
Scholtz Advertising Agency, Los Angeles, CA
Strathmore Apartments, Westwood, CA

1938
Brown House, Fishers Island, NY
Emerson Junior High School, Westwood, CA
Koblick House, Los Angeles, CA
Lewin House, Santa Monica, CA
Schiff and Wolfes Apartment Duplex, San Francisco, CA

1939–1941 ▶ Appointed member and, later, chair (1941–1944) of the California State Planning Board

1939
Davey House, Monterey, CA
Eurich House, Los Altos Heights, CA
Gill House, Glendale, CA
Johnson/Clayton/Stafford Houses, Los Altos, CA
McIntosh House, Los Angeles, CA

National Youth Administration Centers, Sacramento and San Luis Obispo, CA
Scioberetti House, Berkeley, CA
Ward and Berger House, Los Angeles, CA

1940
Dr. Grant Beckstrand House, Palos Verdes, CA
Evans Plywood Building, Lebanon, OR
De Graaf House, Portland, OR
Hauswirth House, Berkeley, CA
Kahn House, San Francisco, CA
Sweet House, Glendale, CA

1941
Howard and Lois Bald House, Ojai, CA
Maxwell House, Los Angeles, CA
Avion Village Housing, Grand Prairie, TX

1942
Bonnet House, Los Angeles, CA
Branch House, Los Angeles, CA
Hacienda Village Housing, Los Angeles, CA
Kelton Apartments, Westwood, CA
Nesbitt House, Los Angeles, CA
Progressive Builders Homes, Burbank, CA
Pueblo del Rio Housing, Los Angeles, CA
Rethy House, Sierra Madre, CA
Van Cleef House, Los Angeles, CA
Channel Heights Housing, San Pedro, CA

1943–1945 ▶ Visiting professor of design at Bennington College, Bennington, Vermont, during wartime building moratorium

1943
Channel Heights Community Center, San Pedro, CA

1944–1945 ▶ Chief architectural and planning consultant, government of Puerto Rico

1945
Rural Health Centers, Puerto Rico
Margolis Stores, Palm Springs, CA

1946
Ayeroff Brothers Store, Los Angeles, CA
Bekey Factory, Los Angeles, CA

Norman Clinic, San Pedro, CA
Hughes Auto Showroom, Los Angeles, CA

1947
Kaufmann House, Palm Springs, CA
Norwalk Service Station, Bakersfield, CA
Schmidt House, Pasadena, CA
Sinay House, Beverly Hills, CA

1948 ▶ Publishes *Architecture of Social Concern in Regions of Mild Climate*
Aloe Health Building, Los Angeles, CA
Atwell House, El Cerrito, CA
Case Study House #20 (Bailey House), Pacific Palisades, CA
Goodson House, Los Angeles, CA
Holiday House Apartments, Malibu Beach, CA
Kievman Apartments, Westwood, CA
Sokol House, Los Angeles, CA
Tremaine House, Montecito, CA
Treweek House, Los Angeles, CA
Tuta House, Palos Verdes, CA

1949–1958 ▶ Partnership with Robert E. Alexander, Neutra and Alexander

1949
Chase House, Santa Barbara, CA
Freedman House, Los Angeles, CA
Greenberg House, Los Angeles, CA
Hines House, Palos Verdes, CA
Mill Creek Summit Maintenance Yard, Mill Creek, CA
Rourke House, Beverly Hills, CA
Wilkins House, South Pasadena, CA

1950 ▶ Exhibition at the Museo de Arte Moderna, São Paulo, Brazil. From now until his death, receives a steady stream of honors, gold medals, honorary doctorates and prizes, including the Cross of the Republic of Germany, 1967; the Gold Ring, City of Vienna, 1968; and the Gold Medal, A.I.A., 1977.
Beckstrand Mountain Lodge, Meadow, UT
Coe House, Palos Verdes, CA
ED-AL Jewish Community Center, Montebello, CA
Rathburn House, Los Angeles, CA
Kun House #2, Los Angeles, CA
Neutra Office Building, Los Angeles, CA

Dion Neutra/Reunion House, Los Angeles, CA
Northwestern Mutual Fire Association
Building, Los Angeles, CA
O'Brien House, Shreveport, LA
Orange Coast College Swim Stadium, Costa
Mesa, CA
Sanders House, Palos Verdes, CA
Wirin House, Los Angeles, CA

1951
Brod House, Arcadia, CA
Everist House, Sioux City, IA
Fischer House, Spokane, WA
Goldman House, Encino, CA
Helburn Residence, Bozeman, MT
Heryford House, Los Angeles, CA
Hinds House, Los Angeles, CA
Hunter House, Los Angeles, CA
Kester Avenue School, Los Angeles, CA
Logar House, Granada Hills, CA
Meltzer House, Los Angeles, CA
Mosby House, Missoula, MT
Miller House, Los Angeles, CA
Nelson House, Orinda, CA

1952
Adelup School, Adelup Point, Guam
Auerbacher Mountain Lodge, Luring Pines, CA
Goodman House, San Bernardino, CA
Heller House, Beverly Hills, CA
Marshall House, Rancho Santa Fe, CA
Matlock House, Long Beach, CA
McElwain House, Reseda, CA
Miller House, El Cerito, CA
Moore House, Ojai, CA
Van Sicklen House, Rancho Santa Fe, CA

1953
Auerbacher House, Redlands, CA
Beckstrand Medical Clinic, Long Beach, CA
Eagle Rock Park Clubhouse, Los Angeles, CA
Elliot House, Bedford, OH
Governor's House, Agana, Guam
Haefely and Moore Houses, Long Beach, CA
Hall House, Newport Beach, CA
Kramer House, Norco, CA
Moore House, Manhattan Beach, CA
Orange Coast College Buildings, Costa
Mesa, CA

**Richard Neutra with the photographer Julius
Shulman, 1950**

Price House, Bayport, NY
San Bernardino Medical Center, San
Bernardino, CA
Schaarman House, Los Angeles, CA

1954 ▶ *Survival through Design*, Neutra's most
important philosophical treatise, is published by
Oxford University Press.
Hammerman House, West Los Angeles, CA
Kesler House, Pacific Palisades, CA
Weston House, Los Angeles, CA

1955
Air Force Housing, Mountain Home, ID
Brown House, Bel Air, CA
Corwin House, Weston, CT
Gemological Institute of America, Los Angeles, CA
Hansch House, Claremont, CA
Kronish House, Beverly Hills, CA
Logar Store, Granada Hills, CA
Perkins House, Pasadena, CA
Roberts House, Covina, CA
Serulnic House, Tujunga, CA
Staller House, Los Angeles, CA
Weihe House, Portuguese Bend, CA

1956
Adler House, Brentwood, CA
Amalgamated Clothing Workers of America Union
Building, Los Angeles, CA
Artega House, San Fernando, CA
Chuey House, Los Angeles, CA

Cohen House, Malibu, CA
Kilbury House, Palos Verdes, CA
Livingston House, Chattanooga, TN
Miller House, Norristown, PA
Crawford House, Hillsborough, CA
De Schulthess House, Havana, Cuba
Slavin House, Santa Barbara, CA
Troxell House, Los Angeles, CA

1957
Alamitos-Lawrence Intermediate School,
Garden Grove, CA
Clark House, Pasadena, CA
Ferro Chemical Company, Bedford, OH
Gillen House, San Bernardino, CA
Hacienda Motor Hotel, San Pedro, CA
Hillcrest School, location unkown
Miramar Naval Station Chapel, Miramar, CA
Nash House, Camarillo, CA
Sorrells House, Shoshone, CA
Wise House, San Pedro, CA
Yew House, Los Angeles, CA

1958 ▶ Exhibition at the UCLA Art Gallery,
University of California, Los Angeles, CA
Cole House, La Habra, CA
Connell House, Carmel, CA
Flavin House, Los Angeles, CA
Friedland House, Gladwyn, PA
Hassrick House, Philadelphia, PA
Huebsch House, Monterey Park, CA
Hughes House, Los Angeles, CA
Kraigher House #2, Litchfield, CT
Lavers Office Building, Tulare, CA
Leddy House, Bakersfield, CA
Oxley House, La Jolla, CA
Rados House, San Pedro, CA
Riviera Methodist Church, Torrance, CA
St. John's College Art & Science Building,
Annapolis, MD
UCLA Experimental and Training School,
Westwood, CA

1959 ▶ Exhibition at Kunstgewerbemuseum,
Zurich
California State University Fine Arts Building,
Northridge, CA
Claremont Methodist Church, Claremont, CA
Crescent Professional Building, West Hollywood, CA

Dailey House, Palos Verdes, CA
Dayton Planetarium, Dayton, OH
Larsen House, Calabasas, CA
Lew House, Los Angeles, CA
Loring House, Los Angeles, CA
McSorley House, Thousand Oaks, CA
National Charity League Administration Building,
Los Angeles, CA
Ninneman House, Claremont, CA
Oyler House, Lone Pine, CA
Pariser House, Uniontown, PA
Singleton House, Los Angeles, CA
United States Embassy, Karachi, West Pakistan
Warner House, Chesterton, IN

1960
Bell House, Santa Barbara, CA
Bewobau Housing, Quickborn and Walldorf,
Germany
Bizzari House, Cincinnati, OH
Bond House, San Diego, CA
Coveney House, King of Prussia, PA
Glen House, Stamford, CT
Inadomi House, Los Angeles, CA
Kambara House, Los Angeles, CA
Pickering House, Lido Isle, Newport Beach, CA
Quandt House, Apple Valley, CA
Sale House, Los Angeles, CA

1961
Apartment House, Washington, DC
Buena Park Swim Stadium, Buena Park, CA
Cytron House, Beverly Hills, CA
Field House, Encino, CA
Gettysburg Cyclorama Center, Gettysburg, PA
Hailey House, Los Angeles, CA
Lemoore Naval Air Base Housing, Lemoore, CA
Richard J. Neutra School, Lemoore, CA
Levitt House, Beverly Hills, CA
Linn House, Los Angeles, CA
List House, Grand Rapids, MI
Oberholzer House, Rolling Hills, Palos Verdes, CA
Ohara House, Los Angeles, CA
Painted Desert Visitors' Center, Painted Desert, AZ
Palos Verdes High School, Palos Verdes, CA
Rang House, Königstein im Taunus, Germany
Santa Ana Police Facilities, Santa Ana, CA
Simpson College Buildings, Indianola, IA
Tiffany House, Lemoore, CA

United Auto Workers Building, Pico Rivera, CA
University of Nevada Arts Center, Reno, NV
Casa Tuia, Ascona, Switzerland

1962
Akai House, Los Angeles, CA
Erman House, Encino, CA
Garden Grove Community Church, Garden Grove,
CA
Goldman House, Des Moines, IA
Gonzales-Gorrondona House, Caracas, Venezuela
Hendershot House, Los Angeles, CA
Hrabe House, Calabasas, CA
County of Los Angeles Hall of Records, Los
Angeles, CA
Maslon House, Cathedral City, CA
Pitcairn House, Bryn Athyn, PA
Stone-Fisher Platform Houses, Los Angeles, CA

Sketch of Dione by Richard Neutra

1963 ▶ VDL I is destroyed by fire; guesthouse
survives. Rebuilt the following years under the
supervision of Dion and codesigned by Dion and
his father.
Adelphi University Swirbul Library, Garden City,
Long Island, NY
Grelling House, Ascona, Switzerland

Mariners Medical Arts Center, Newport Beach, CA
U.S.C. Child Guidance Clinic, Los Angeles, CA

1964
Adelphi University Building Administration
Department, Garden City, NY
Kuhns House, Woodland Hills, CA
Poster Apartments, Los Angeles, CA
Rentsch House, Wengen, Switzerland
Taylor House, Glendale, CA

1965–1970 ▶ Partnership with son Dion, Richard
and Dion Neutra

1965
Congregational Church School, Hacienda
Heights, CA
Reno-Sparks Convention Center, Reno, NV
Rice House, Loch Island, Richmond, VA
Roberson Memorial Center, Binghampton, NY
St. Andrew Methodist Church, Santa Maria, CA

1966
Bucerius House, Navegna, Switzerland
Tower of Hope, Garden Grove, CA
La Veta Medical Building, Orange, CA
VDL Research House II, Los Angeles, CA
Roland von Huene Cabin, Mammoth, CA

1967
Kemper House, Wuppertal, Germany
Shinoda House, Santa Barbara, CA

1968
Brown House, Washington, DC
Claremont Methodist Church Extension,
Claremont, CA
Guenter Pescher House, Wuppertal, Germany
Orange County Courthouse, Santa Ana, CA
Stern House, Beverly Hills, CA

1969
Marcel Delcourt House, Croix, France
University of Pennsylvania Graduate
Student Housing, Philadelphia, PA

1970 ▶ Dies of heart attack on April 16 at his
client's home, the Kemper House

California

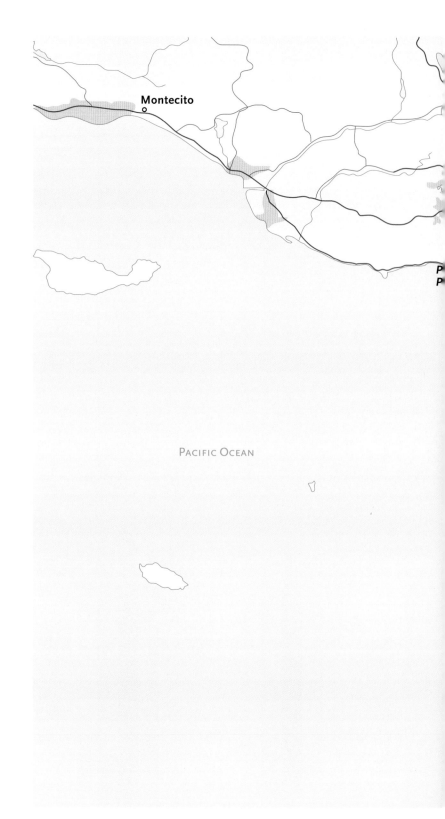

Montecito

PACIFIC OCEAN

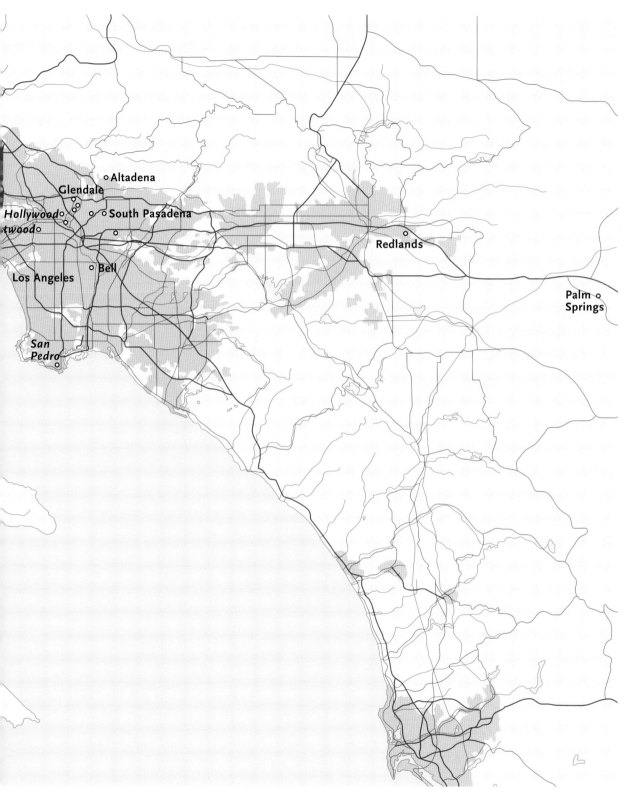

Altadena

Glendale

Hollywood

twood

South Pasadena

Redlands

Los Angeles

Bell

Palm
Springs

San
Pedro

Bibliography

Credits

Books by Neutra

▶ Wie baut Amerika. Julius Hoffman Verlag, Stuttgart, 1927.
▶ Amerika. Die Stilbildung des neuen Bauens in den Vereinigten Staaten. Anton Schroll Verlag, Vienna, 1930.
▶ Architecture of Social Concern in Regions of Mild Climate. Gert Todtmann, São Paulo, 1948.
▶ Mysteries and Realities of the Site. Willard Morgan, Scarsdale, 1951.
▶ Survival through Design. Oxford University Press, New York, 1954.
▶ Realismo Biológico: Un nuevo Renacimiento humanístico en arquitectura. Editorial Nueva Visión, Buenos Aires, 1958.
▶ Life and Shape: The Autobiography of Richard Neutra. Appleton-Century-Crofts, New York, 1962.
▶ World and Dwelling. Alexander Koch Verlag, Stuttgart, 1962.
▶ Naturnahes Bauen. Alexander Koch Verlag, Stuttgart, 1970.
▶ Planzen, Wasser, Steine, Licht. Parey Verlag, Berlin, 1974. By Richard and Dion Neutra.
▶ Nature Near: Late Essays of Richard Neutra. Edited by William Marlin. Capra Press, Santa Barbara, 1989.

Books about Neutra

▶ Boesiger, Willy: Richard Neutra: Buildings and Projects. Girsberger Verlag, Zurich, 1951.
▶ Boesiger, Willy: Richard Neutra: Buildings and Projects, 1950–1960. Girsberger Verlag, Zurich, 1959.
▶ Boesiger, Willy: Richard Neutra: Buildings and Projects, 1961–1966. Girsberger Verlag, Zurich, 1966.
▶ Drexler, Arthur, and Thomas S. Hines: The Architecture of Richard Neutra. From International Style to California Modern. The Museum of Modern Art, New York, 1982.
▶ Exner, Hermann: Richard Neutra, Bauen und die Sinneswelt. Verlag der Kunst, Dresden, 1977.
▶ Ford, Edward R.: The Details of Modern Architecture, vol. 2, 1928 to 1988. MIT Press, Cambridge, MA, and London, 1996.
▶ Hines, Thomas S.: Richard Neutra and the Search for Modern Architecture. Oxford University Press, New York, 1982.
▶ Koeper, Frederick: The Richard and Dion Neutra VDL Research House I and II. California State Polytechnic University, Pomona, 1985.
▶ Lamprecht, Barbara: Richard Neutra: Complete Works. Taschen Publications, Cologne, 2000.
▶ McCoy, Esther: Richard Neutra. George Braziller, New York, 1960.
▶ McCoy, Esther: Vienna to Los Angeles: Two journeys: Letters between R. M. Schindler and Richard Neutra. Art + Architecture Press, Santa Monica, 1979.
▶ Neumann, Dietrich (ed.): Richard Neutra's Windshield House. Harvard University Graduate School of Design, Harvard University Art Museum, Cambridge, MA, and Yale University Press, New Haven, CT, and London, 2001.
▶ Neutra, Dione: Richard Neutra: Promise and Fulfillment, 1919–1932. Southern Illinois University Press, Carbondale, 1986.
▶ Sack, Manfred: Richard Neutra. Foreword by Dion Neutra. Artemis Verlag, Zurich, 1992.

Images copyright permission courtesy Dion Neutra, architect, on behalf of Neutra Estate.

▶ Boesiger, Willy: Richard Neutra: Buildings and Projects. Girsberger Verlag, Zurich, 1951: pp. 4, 41 (bottom)
▶ College of Environmental Design, California State University Pomona: pp. 11, 18 (top and bottom), 19, 31, 33 (l.), 36, 37 (top), 38 (top), 39, 86, 87, 88, 89 (r.), 90
▶ Eva Fleckenstein, Bremen: pp. 26 (bottom l. and r.), 29, 33 (top and bottom r.), 34 (bottom), 37 (bottom), 40 (bottom l. and r.), 43, 48 (bottom l. and r.), 52 (top), 59 (bottom), 65 (bottom), 67 (l.), 72 (bottom l.), 75 (top l.), 77 (bottom), 81 (bottom), 84 (top, center and bottom r.), 89 (top)
▶ David Glomb, Rancho Mirage, California: pp. 58 (top), 59 (top), 70, 72 (bottom r.), 73 (top and bottom)
▶ Gössel und Partner, Bremen: 94/95
▶ Don Higgins Photography, Santa Monica, California: 92
▶ Julius Shulman: pp. 2, 6, 8, 10, 12, 13, 14 (top), 15, 24, 27, 28, 30, 34 (top), 40 (top), 42, 44, 45 (top), 46, 47, 48 (top l. and r.), 50, 51, 52 (l., center and r.), 53, 56, 58 (bottom), 60, 61, 62, 64, 65 (top l.), 66, 67 (r.), 68, 69, 74, 75 (bottom l. and top l.), 76, 77 (top l. and r.), 78, 79, 82, 83, 84 (l.), 85
▶ © G. E. Kidder Smith / Corbis: p. 49
▶ Department of Special Collection, Charles E. Young Research Library, UCLA: pp. 9, 14 (bottom), 16, 20, 21, 25, 32, 35, 38 (bottom), 41 (top), 45 (bottom), 54, 55, 65 (top r.), 72 (top), 93
▶ photography by Tim Street-Porter: pp. 22, 23, 26 (top), 80, 81 (top)